The AI Business Enablement Audit

The Operating System for Running AI as a Permanent Business Function

Stephen R. Jordan

SRJ Consulting & Services Publishing

Copyright

The AI Business Enablement Audit™

The Operating System for Running AI as a Permanent Business Function

The Operating Discipline for AI Library™, Volume I

Pillar I: AI Business Services™

Volumes are numbered by operating sequence, the natural order in which the disciplines build inside a business.

Published by SRJ Consulting & Services Publishing, Frisco, Texas

SRJConsultingServices.com

Names: Jordan, Stephen R. (Stephen Ray), 1960- author.

Title: The AI business enablement audit : the operating system for running AI as a permanent business function / Stephen R. Jordan.

Description: [Frisco, Texas] : SRJ Consulting & Services Publishing, [2026] | Series: Operating discipline for AI library ; v. 1. | Includes bibliographical references.

Identifiers: ISBN: 9798996565801 (Paperback) | 9798996565818 (Hardback) | 9798996565825 (eBook)

Subjects: LCSH: Artificial intelligence--Economic aspects. | Artificial intelligence--Industrial applications. | Industrial management--Technological innovations. | Management--Technological innovations. | Business enterprises--Technological innovations. | Information technology--Management. | Decision making. | Risk assessment. | Strategic planning. | Leadership. | BISAC: BUSINESS & ECONOMICS / Information Management. | BUSINESS & ECONOMICS / Management. | COMPUTERS / Artificial Intelligence / General.

Classification: LCC: HD30.2 .J67 2026 | DDC: 658/.0563--dc23

Trademarks

Disclaimer

This book provides general operational and management frameworks intended to support executive decision-making. It is sold with the understanding that neither the author nor the publisher is rendering legal, financial, regulatory, compliance, tax, or technical advice specific to any organization or situation.

References to specific laws, regulations, standards, and frameworks — including the NIST AI Risk Management Framework, ISO/IEC 42001, SOC 2, HIPAA, GLBA, and applicable state laws — are provided for general operational guidance only. The legal and regulatory environment around AI continues to develop rapidly, and the requirements applicable to any organization depend on its industry, geography, customer base, and operational context. The frameworks described may not be suitable for every circumstance. If professional advice is required, the services of a competent professional should be sought.

Case examples in this book are composites drawn from consulting engagements; identifying details have been abstracted. Any resemblance to a specific organization is unintended.

Neither the author nor the publisher shall be liable for any loss of profit or any other commercial damages — including but not limited to special, incidental, consequential, or other damages — arising directly or indirectly from the use or application of any information contained in this work.

AI Disclosure

This book was produced with AI assistance. The text was developed through extensive use of AI tools, with substantial editorial review, structural revision, and final approval by the author. All figures, diagrams, scorecards, and illustrations were generated using AI tools under the direction of the author, who reviewed and approved each one for accuracy and appropriateness. The author retains full responsibility for the content, analysis, frameworks, judgments, and conclusions presented in this work. The book is an original English-language work; no portion was machine-translated from another language.

Cover design by Muhammad Shakir Tahir, Book Bloom Studio

First Edition

Dedication

For the operators, the people who do the work of running the business rather than the work of talking about running it.

Acknowledgments

This book is the product of more than two decades of operational work across accounting, enterprise technology, cybersecurity, and consulting practice. Many of the situations described in these pages, with identifying details abstracted, emerged from engagements with business owners and executive teams who allowed me into the reality of how AI was, and was not, being managed inside their companies. Their candor made the framework possible. The case patterns presented as Northpoint Advisors, Meridian Manufacturing, and the other composite examples reflect their experience, not their identities.

The academic literature on AI adoption, organizational readiness, governance maturity, and operational integration has matured rapidly over the past five years. The references collected at the end of this volume represent a portion of the body of work that shaped my thinking. Particular acknowledgment is owed to the researchers whose empirical and conceptual contributions appear throughout this text, and to the broader community of scholars whose work continues to clarify what AI governance actually requires inside operating organizations.

Thanks are due to the executive peers and operating colleagues who challenged the framework before it reached publication, the consulting clients who tested its earliest drafts in working engagements, and Shakir, whose visual judgment shaped how this book first reaches its reader.

The errors that remain are mine.

Stephen R. Jordan

Frisco, Texas

2026

Executive Summary

AI is already inside your business. It is drafting your emails, pricing your proposals, screening your résumés, and answering your customers — whether leadership signed off on any of it or not. The question is no longer whether to adopt AI. The question is whether anyone in your building can tell you what it is doing.

For most owners and executives I work with, the honest answer is no. They cannot list every AI tool in active use. They cannot say what those tools cost in total. They cannot describe what data those tools are touching, or who in the company is responsible for the outputs those tools produce. None of that is a sign of failure. It is the predictable consequence of a technology that arrived through hundreds of small decisions made below the leadership line — a vendor adding a feature here, an employee subscribing to a tool there, a software platform quietly turning on AI capabilities in its next release.

This book is the system that catches up.

The framework is called The AI Operating System™, and it manages AI the way a competent business manages any other consequential function — with visibility into what exists, accountability for what it produces, controls on what it costs, and a recurring rhythm of review. At its center sits The AI Business Enablement Audit™, a five-dimension assessment that lets a non-technical leadership team see — usually for the first time — what AI is actually doing inside their company, what it is worth, and where it is exposing the business.

This is not a technology book. It is a management book about a technology. It does not require an engineering background, an IT department, or a six-figure software investment. It requires the same discipline you already apply to your finances, your hiring, and your compliance. Bring that discipline to AI and the rest of the work becomes tractable.

By the end of the book you will have an inventory of every AI system operating in your company, a real cost picture, a performance baseline, a written governance policy, and a recurring review rhythm that keeps the whole system honest. More importantly, you will have stopped reacting to AI and started running it.

Contents

Introduction

You're Not Behind — You're Just Operating Without a System

A few months ago, I sat down with the founder of a mid-sized professional services firm. Smart operator, twenty-five years in the business, the kind of executive who can quote his firm's revenue per partner from memory. He told me he was worried his company had fallen behind on AI. I asked him a simpler question: how many AI tools were currently in use across his organization?

He guessed three. Maybe four if you counted the writing assistant his marketing director liked.

We found nineteen.

That gap, between what leadership believes is happening with AI and what is actually happening, is the most common condition I encounter in my consulting work. It is also the central premise of this book. The owners and executives I meet are not behind on AI. AI has already arrived in their companies. The problem is that no one has written the rules for how it operates inside the business.

Those are very different problems. Being behind means ground has been permanently lost. Operating without a system means there is no framework yet in place to create visibility and control. The first problem is mostly unfixable. The second is entirely fixable, usually with the people and processes already in the building.

This is the situation most businesses are in today, whether or not leadership has named it. Employees are using AI tools they found on their own to do work faster. Software vendors are bundling AI capabilities into platforms the company already pays for. Automation features are being switched on through routine updates that no one reads. The tools influence customer communications, hiring decisions, financial reports, and the daily work of nearly every department, and almost none of that activity is being tracked.

Compare AI to any other consequential function in your business. You probably have a closing process for the books, an approval chain for major expenses, a written policy on customer data, a hiring workflow, a procurement standard. AI has none of that in most companies. It has been allowed to operate inside the business without the basic management infrastructure that every other function takes for granted. That is the gap this book is built to close.

I have spent more than twenty years watching this pattern play out in different forms, in accounting departments, in enterprise security teams, in operational consulting engagements, in incident response work. Technology gets adopted faster than anyone bothers to govern it, and the bill arrives later. The bill might be regulatory exposure. It might be a quiet decline in output quality. It might be a five-figure annual subscription that no one can account for. AI is the most recent version of the pattern, and it is moving faster than the ones that came before.

The good news is that the fix is not technical. You do not need a machine-learning team to govern AI. You do not need to understand how a model is trained to decide who in your company is responsible for the output the model produces. What you need is the management discipline you already bring to finance, hiring, and compliance — and a framework built specifically to apply that discipline to AI.

That framework is what the rest of this book provides.

Figure I.1 — The Unmanaged AI Environment

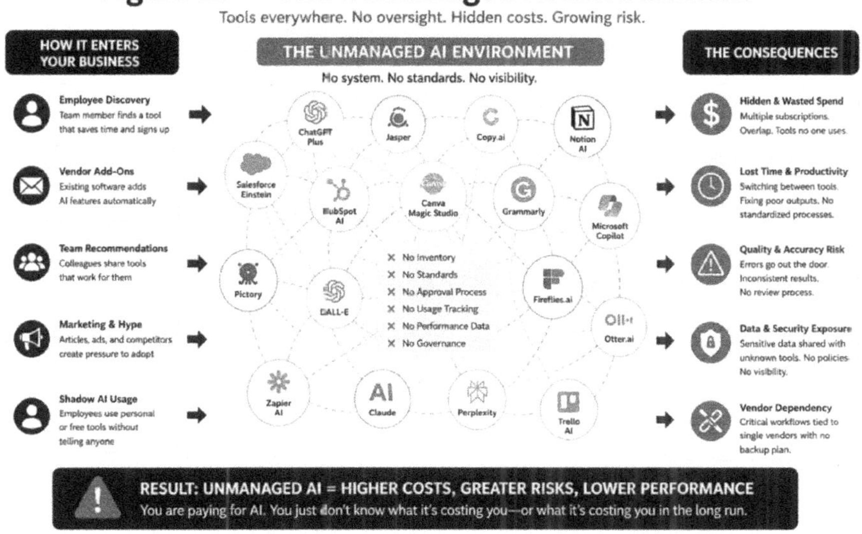

When AI is run inside a deliberate system, leadership recovers visibility. The company can answer the questions every executive ought to be able to answer: what AI tools are we running, what are they costing us, what value they are producing, and what risks are they introducing. With those answers, decisions become easier, faster, and defensible. Without them, decisions are guesses.

This book is built for the executive who wants to make decisions rather than guesses.

What You're Going to Learn — And Why This Book Is Different

Most books written about AI fall into one of two camps. The first explains how the technology works — neural networks, transformers, the long road to artificial general intelligence. The second offers tactical productivity advice — prompts to copy, shortcuts to try, lists of tools that will save you an hour a day. Both have their place. Neither solves the problem this book is built around.

This is a management book. It treats AI the way a serious business already treats finance, hiring, vendor risk, and compliance — as a function that requires visibility, ownership, controls, and a regular review cadence. The goal is not to make you an expert in the technology. The goal is to make you the person in the room who can answer the four questions every executive ought to be able to answer about AI inside their company:

- What tools are running?
- What are they costing us — fully loaded?
- What value are they producing — measurably?
- What risks are they introducing — and who is responsible for those risks?

If you can answer those four questions today with documentation rather than estimates, you do not need this book. In my consulting work, fewer than one in ten leadership teams can.

The diagnostic engine at the center of the framework is the AI Business Enablement Audit™ — a five-dimension review that runs through tools, costs, performance, risk, and alignment. Most companies have never done anything like it. The first time they do, the picture they find is rarely catastrophic and almost always surprising. I have yet to run an audit in which the leadership team's pre-audit estimate of AI spend matched the actual number. The actual number is usually two to four times higher, and the breakdown of where the money is going is rarely where they expected.

From the audit, the book moves into the work that follows it, building a cost control structure, putting performance measurement in place, writing real governance policy, defining ownership for AI-produced outputs, and standing up a review rhythm that does not collapse under normal business pressure. Each piece is independently useful. Together they form a working operating system.

One thing this book will not do is recommend specific tools, rank platforms, or take a position on which vendor's chatbot is best. That ground is fully covered elsewhere, the answers change every quarter, and they will be obsolete before this book reaches its second printing. The framework here is intentionally tool-agnostic. It works for the company running ChatGPT Enterprise and the company that has never paid for an AI subscription in its life, because in both companies, AI is already operating, and in both companies, the management work is the same.

When this is done well, AI changes behavior inside the business. It stops behaving like a fashion. It starts behaving like a managed function. Decisions about new tools become deliberate. Performance becomes measurable. Risk becomes visible before it becomes a problem. That shift begins the moment the business decides to run AI as a system rather than as a collection of independent experiments.

A Map of the Journey Ahead

Before we go further, a brief tour of how the book is organized — because the chapter order matters, and the framework is designed to be read in sequence.

Chapter 1 makes the case that doing nothing about AI is not a neutral choice. It costs money, leaks risk and erodes control quietly enough that most leadership teams do not register it until something forces them to. This is the chapter to give the colleague who is still treating AI as someone else's problem.

Chapter 2 is about Shadow AI, the AI in your business right now that no one approved. It explains where it comes from, why employees use it (usually for good reasons), and how to bring it into the light without launching a witch hunt.

Chapters 3 through 5 walk through the AI Business Enablement Audit — the diagnostic that makes the rest of the book operable. By the end of the audit, you will know what tools you have, what you are paying for, and how to think about both. For many leadership teams this is the first audit of its kind they have ever run on AI specifically. The visibility it produces is, in my consulting experience, the single most valuable hour of work in the entire framework.

Chapters 6 through 9 take that visibility and turn it into management infrastructure: performance measurement (Chapter 6), risk controls (Chapter 7), written governance (Chapter 8), and strategic alignment with your actual business goals (Chapter 9). These are the chapters where the system gets its teeth

Chapters 10 and 11 deal with the work that decides whether the system actually changes how your business operates: integrating AI into real workflows (Chapter 10) and building a repeatable decision model for every future AI choice the business has to make (Chapter 11).

Chapter 12 brings everything together as a running operating system, the recurring rhythm of review, audit, and adjustment that keeps the framework honest over time. The conclusion describes what the business looks like after twelve months of running the system, and what it looks like for competitors who do not.

Every chapter ends with a section called Putting It into Practice, a short, concrete sequence the reader can apply inside their own business immediately. The framework is built for working executives, not for theorists. Anything that could not be implemented by a leadership team operating under normal constraints, meaning limited budget, limited staff, and no dedicated AI team, was either rewritten or cut.

A note on who this book is for. It is written for owners, presidents, CFOs, COOs, and operating partners at small and mid-sized businesses — companies between roughly twenty and a thousand employees. It is also useful for larger organizations whose AI work is still happening at the function or division level. It assumes you are smart, busy, financially literate, and uninterested in being talked down to. It does not assume you have any background in AI.

Every framework, worksheet, and template referenced in this book is available as a working document at **srjconsultingservices.com/library/enablement**. Bring them into a leadership meeting, a budget review, or a board discussion and use them directly. This is Volume I of *The Operating Discipline for AI Library*, a nine-volume series covering the full operating discipline required to govern AI as a business capability — from initial audit through readiness, governance, efficiency, and security. The volumes are numbered to reflect the operating sequence in which the disciplines build on each other inside a business. The complete library and the release schedule for forthcoming volumes are at **srjconsultingservices.com/library**. Let's begin.

Chapter 1: The Unmanaged AI Problem

Why Most Businesses Are Already Losing

CHAPTER OUTCOMES

At the end of this chapter, you will be able to:

- Explain why unmanaged AI is already creating hidden costs, risks, and missed opportunities.
- Identify the financial, operational, and reputational consequences of doing nothing.
- Use the three essential questions (visibility, cost, results) to assess your current AI management maturity.
- Recognize the gap between leadership awareness and employee AI adoption (shadow AI) and why it matters.
- Understand why most AI initiatives fail to deliver value without the right management infrastructure.
- Commit to leading AI deliberately by establishing the foundation for an AI governance operating system.

The Hidden Cost of Doing Nothing

Most owners I talk to think of "not having an AI strategy" as a defensible position. They are waiting. The technology is still maturing. The competition does not appear to be running away. There is no urgency yet.

Inaction is not a strategy. It is a different strategy, and it has costs.

While leadership waits, the company itself does not. Employees adopt tools to do work faster. Software vendors switch on AI features in platforms the business already pays for. Automation creeps into reports, contracts, customer emails, and internal communications. The technology does not need leadership's approval to enter the business; it has already entered the business. The absence of a strategy does not prevent that. It just means the expansion happens without anyone watching it (Hansen et al., 2024).

The consequences are rarely loud. Unmanaged AI does not announce itself. It accumulates — slowly enough that no quarterly review flags it, expensively enough that by the time someone notices, the company is already dependent on systems it never formally evaluated. That is the pattern I have watched play out across more than thirty client engagements. The shape of the problem is always the same: a leadership team is genuinely surprised by what the audit surfaces, because the technology spread through hundreds of small decisions that individually were too minor to track.

Consider what those decisions look like in practice. A marketing manager subscribes to a generative writing tool to draft campaign copy. A finance lead pastes an income statement into an AI assistant to get a one-page summary for the board. A salesperson installs a browser extension that rewrites prospect emails before they go out. A vendor pushes a software update that adds an AI "smart suggestions" feature to the helpdesk platform — nobody opts in; nobody opts out; the feature is just on. Each decision is rational at the individual level. None of them gets reviewed against the others, against the company's data policies, or against the budget.

The financial impact builds the same way. Costs accumulate through monthly subscriptions, premium tiers, seat additions, usage-based overages, and bundled feature upgrades that vendors slip into existing contracts. Because each charge is small in isolation, most never trigger the scrutiny that a six-figure software purchase would. Ask the CFO what the company spends on AI in total — across every department, every credit card, every embedded vendor feature. In my consulting work, that question gets a confident answer roughly one time in ten. In the other nine, the real number turns out to be two to four times higher than the estimate.

Cost is the easiest part of the problem to talk about. It is rarely the most expensive part.

AI tools are not passive software running in the background. They produce language that goes to customers. They produce numbers that feed decisions. They shape résumé reviews, contract reviews, and proposal reviews. When that activity is not governed, three things happen quietly:

Sensitive information, financials, customer records, internal documents — gets pasted into platforms whose data-handling terms no one has read.

AI-produced outputs flow into customer communications, hiring decisions, and financial reporting without a defined review step or a named human owner.

Errors that technology routinely produces, confident sounding, but wrong, go uncaught because no review process was designed to catch them.

Damage from this kind of exposure rarely arrives all at once. It arrives as a wrong number in a client deliverable that the client notices first. It arrives as a hiring screen that quietly downranks half the qualified candidate pool. It arrives as an automated email that goes out with the wrong price. None of these events look like an AI failure when it happens. It looks like a normal business mistake, and that is precisely why the underlying cause is so easy to miss. Multiple enterprise studies, including work from McKinsey, Deloitte, and Gartner — have consistently found that most AI initiatives fail to produce measurable business value beyond isolated experiments (Westover, 2025). The most common reason is not the technology. It is the absence of management infrastructure around it.

None of this is inevitable. The fix is not to eliminate AI or to slow it down. The fix is to bring the same management discipline to AI that the business already applies to its other consequential functions: know what exists, know what it costs, know what it produces, and assign someone to be accountable for it. The rest of this chapter is about why those four basics, in this category, are usually missing — and what it costs the business when they are.

The Three Questions Every Business Owner Should Be Able to Answer

FIGURE 1.1

The Three Questions Every Business Owner Should Be Able to Answer

These three questions form the foundation of the AI Business Enablement Audit™.

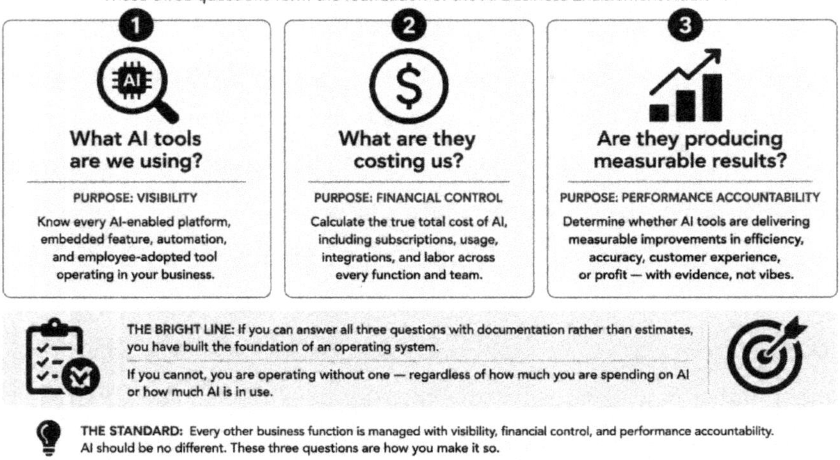

Three questions. They are the most important questions an executive can ask about AI inside their own company. They are also the questions almost no one can answer cleanly on first attempt.

What AI tools are we using? What are they costing us? Are they producing measurable results?

A leadership team that can answer all three with documentation rather than estimates has built the foundation of an operating system. A leadership team that cannot is operating without one — regardless of how much the company is spending on AI or how much AI is in active use. This is the bright line.

The questions sound elementary. They are framed deliberately that way. The same three questions, asked about any other business function, would feel almost absurdly basic. What software are we using? What does it cost? Is it producing results? Most companies could answer those questions in fifteen minutes about their CRM, their accounting platform, their HRIS, or their cloud hosting. The answers are documented. The numbers are budgeted. The performance is tracked. That is the operating standard for every other category of business technology.

AI sits outside that standard in most companies, and the gap is not a technology problem. It is a management problem.

Most owners can name the handful of AI tools they personally use or personally approved. What they cannot name, usually, are the tools their employees adopted independently, the AI features that arrived through software updates in platforms they already paid for, and the subscriptions running on department-level credit cards. The visible layer represents a fraction of what is actually in use. Until the rest is documented, every estimate of total spending, total exposure, and total impact is a guess.

The performance question is harder still. Many leadership teams cannot say, with evidence, whether their AI tools are producing measurable improvements in efficiency, in accuracy, in customer experience, in profit. Tools feel useful. Employees report that they save time. The actual delta is rarely measured. Without benchmarks tied to business outcomes, decisions about whether to keep, expand, or kill a tool come down to vibe. That is a fragile basis for spending decisions of any size.

A scenario I see often: an owner approves a new AI-based document processing tool because it sounds useful and the monthly fee is small. The use case is reasonable. The approval takes three minutes. What no one realizes, because no one has the inventory in front of them — is that two other tools inside the company already perform overlapping functions. Different managers approved each one independently. No one ever compared them. The business is now paying for three subscriptions that solve roughly the same problem, none of them especially well, because none of them have been actively managed against the others.

Situations like that one is the predictable result of decentralized adoption without a structured review framework. The individual decisions are reasonable. The cumulative outcome is not. None of the people involved did anything wrong. The company simply lacked the connecting tissue — the standards, the review process, and the owner-of-record, that would have prevented the overlap.

These three questions form the spine of the audit framework introduced later in this book. They are not diagnostic prompts. They are the management standards the framework is designed to install. When the rest of the book has been put to work, the answers to these questions should be documented, current, and immediately retrievable. That is what running AI as a managed function looks like in practice — and it is the standard the wider research on organizational technology adoption keeps converging on, from different angles (Badghish & Soomro, 2024; Alzahrani, 2025).

How AI Adoption Became AI Chaos

AI did not enter most small and mid-sized businesses through a formal strategy. There was no board memo, no executive decision, no roadmap. AI entered through small decisions made one at a time, in different parts of the company, by people who were just trying to do their jobs better.

In a way, that is a strength of small businesses. They are fast. They have less institutional friction than large enterprises and can adopt new technology in weeks rather than quarters. That speed is an advantage when the rest of the management infrastructure — visibility, governance, oversight — keeps pace with it. When adoption outruns management, the same agility that creates innovation also creates exposure.

The pattern is recognizable once you have seen it a few times. An employee finds a tool that saves time and starts using it. A teammate finds a different tool that does roughly the same thing and uses that one. A vendor releases an update that turns on AI features inside a platform the company has been paying for since 2019, no one signs an updated agreement; the feature just appears. Each step is reasonable. None of them is being tracked.

As adoption widens, the operational picture fragments. One tool becomes five. Five become a dozen. Departments start solving similar problems with different platforms. Costs climb gradually. Outputs vary. Standards diverge. What is forming is not a strategy. It is a set of parallel experiments running in different parts of the company, with no shared measurement and no shared accountability. Research on AI organizational readiness has documented this pattern repeatedly: adoption consistently expands faster than the governance designed to manage it (Sadiq et al., 2021).

Vendor pressure accelerates the dynamic. New AI products launch every week. Sales motions emphasize urgency: competitors are adopting, you are falling behind, pricing changes next month. Industry coverage reinforces the same theme. Under that pressure, leadership teams approve additional tools without first building the infrastructure to oversee the ones they already have. The result is technology adopted faster than the company can absorb it.

A related driver is shadow AI, employees using personal accounts, free platforms, or browser extensions to do work-related tasks. A sales rep uses an AI assistant to summarize calls. An HR coordinator drafts performance reviews in a consumer chatbot. A bookkeeper pastes a P&L into a model to get a quick summary for the partner meeting. The intent is usually innocent. The exposure is not. Recent research has begun to argue, persuasively, that traditional top-down oversight models miss most of this activity entirely; effective governance has to account for individual employee behavior, not just enterprise systems (Hržica et al., 2025). Shadow AI is the subject of Chapter 2, and it gets a fuller treatment there.

It is worth saying clearly: decentralized AI adoption is not, by itself, the problem. In a lot of companies, it is the source of the best operational ideas. Employees who experiment with tools at the edge of their workflow often surface efficiency improvements that leadership would never identify on its own. The issue is not the experimentation. The issue is what happens when experimentation runs without a framework, without an approval path, without a data policy, without a review point. At that stage, useful distributed innovation turns into unmanaged shadow activity, and the business loses the ability to evaluate, govern, or measure any of it.

The way out of this is not to roll any of it back. It is to install the management framework that should have existed alongside the adoption. The chapters ahead are about how to do that without slowing the business down.

The Real Cost You're Not Calculating

Subscription fees are the costs most owners think about when they think about AI. They are also the smallest part of the bill.

The bigger costs hide inside operating hours, error correction, underutilized tools, vendor lock-in, and unmeasured performance. Most of them never show up as line items in accounting software, which is precisely why they are easy to miss.

Lost time and rework. When AI outputs are not consistent or reliable, employees burn hours reviewing and correcting them. When multiple tools with overlapping functions exist across departments, employees burn more time switching between platforms, learning each one's quirks, and reconciling inconsistent outputs. None of this shows up on a P&L. All of it shows up in throughput.

Error cost. AI confidently produces wrong information. Without a review process, those errors move directly into customer emails, financial summaries, hiring decisions, and internal reports. The downstream cost — damaged client relationships, additional labor to fix the mistake, reputational drag, usually exceeds the original subscription by a wide margin. Individual errors are rarely catastrophic. Cumulatively, they are expensive.

Underutilization. Most AI tools are adopted quickly and never reconfigured after the initial setup. Default settings stay default. Prompts stay rushed. The gap between what the tool can do and what employees are using it to do is often enormous. Organizations end up paying full subscription cost for a tiny fraction of the available value

Vendor dependency. AI tools embed into workflows faster than other software categories because the integrations are quick and the productivity gains are immediate. The longer that dependency runs, the harder it gets to unwind. If the vendor changes pricing, modifies terms, throttles features, or shuts down, none of which is hypothetical, the business absorbs the disruption. These dependencies form gradually; the cost of breaking them does not.

Missing performance measurement. Many businesses continue paying for tools without ever determining whether those tools produce measurable value. Productivity feels improved. Tasks feel faster. The actual return is rarely quantified. That gap between perceived performance and measurable performance is one of the most consistent findings in AI cost reviews (Poon et al., 2025). It is also one of the most expensive.

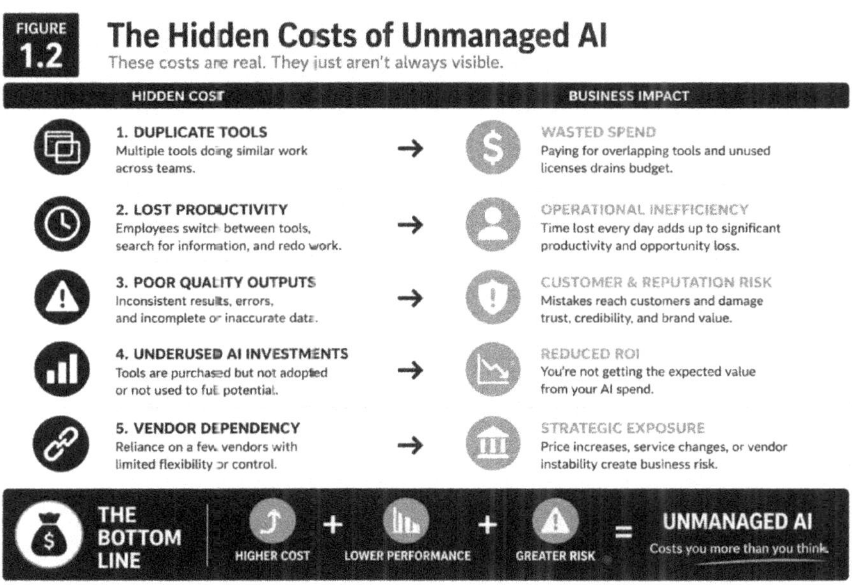

Add it all up and the total cost of unmanaged AI is consistently several multiples of the subscription line. The reason most businesses underestimate it is not denial — it is visibility. The costs that are easy to see are not the ones that matter most. Until the harder costs become visible, the cost picture is fictional. Chapter 5 walks through how to surface them.

What Controlled AI Adoption Actually Looks Like

Most organizations have only ever experienced AI in its fragmented form, and after a while, fragmentation starts to feel like normal. It is not. It is the absence of management, not a management style.

Controlled AI adoption is not a more elaborate version of the same thing. It is a different operating posture. It is also not technically complicated — none of what follows requires an engineering team or a data science group. It requires structure, applied consistently. Research on organizational AI maturity has reinforced this point repeatedly: visibility, leadership oversight, governance, and accountability put in place earlier in the adoption cycle are the strongest predictors of sustainable AI outcomes (Papagiannidis et al., 2022).

In a controlled AI environment, the company maintains a living inventory of every AI tool in active use. Not a one-time spreadsheet, an actively maintained document that gets reviewed on a defined cadence. Each tool on the list has an owner, a cost, a documented purpose, and a way to evaluate whether it is working.

New tools enter the inventory through a defined review process. Before anyone enters a credit card, the proposed tool gets evaluated against the same set of criteria every time: what business outcome it is expected to produce, what it will cost fully loaded, what data it will touch, what risks it introduces, and who will own it. The review is not bureaucratic. In a well-run company it takes thirty minutes. But it happens every time, and it produces a defensible decision.

Spending is visible at the leadership level, total AI spend, by department, by vendor, by category — and reviewed on the same cadence as every other significant expense category. Surprise charges, ghost subscriptions, and silent escalations get caught early rather than discovered during the audit twelve months later.

Performance gets measured. Not exhaustively, but consistently. Every active tool is tied to a specific operational outcome: time saved per task, errors reduced, customer response time improved, revenue activity supported. The measurement does not have to be elaborate. It does have to exist. If a tool cannot demonstrate value against its stated outcome within a defined window, leadership has a defensible basis for deciding whether to fix it, replace it, or retire it. Tools do not stay funded by inertia.

Risk is governed by policy, not by judgment. Employees know what information can and cannot be entered into external AI platforms because the company has written that down and trained on it. New tools require approval before they touch business data. Vendor terms get reviewed before, not after, the company is dependent on the vendor.

Decisions about new tools are made against a consistent standard — cost, value, fit, performance expectations, risk, rather than against the urgency of the marketing pitch that introduced them. Over time, that consistency moves AI from a collection of disconnected experiments into a coordinated function inside the business.

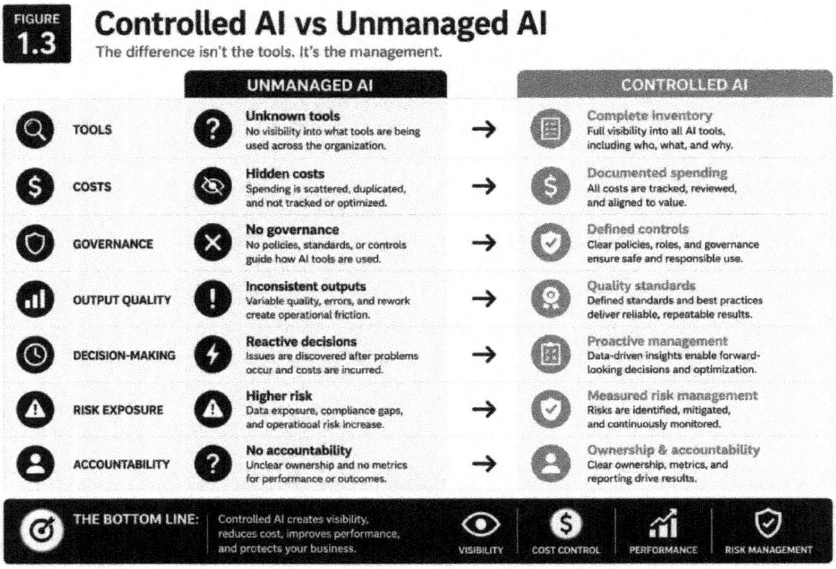

This is not an aspirational picture for large enterprises. It is the achievable standard for any business that decides to install the framework. The next several chapters walk through how to do that. None of it requires a technology background. All of it requires the same discipline you already bring to functions you take more seriously.

Your Starting Point: Taking Stock Before You Build

The gap between where most businesses operate today and where they need to be is smaller than it looks. The constraint is visibility; leadership cannot manage what it cannot see. Before anything else can happen, the company needs an honest baseline.

The baseline starts with the obvious. Open a working document and list every AI-related tool currently known to exist inside the business. Do not stop debating whether a given tool fully qualifies as "AI." If it includes automation, machine learning, generative capability, or AI-powered features that influence work, include it. The list will be incomplete the first time through. That is expected and useful.

Next, look at the financial side. Pull the last six months of credit card statements and subscription records. Look for recurring charges connected to AI platforms, automation tools, or features the business may have agreed to inside larger software contracts. Many of these charges are easy to skim past because they are small individually. Add each one to the inventory with its monthly and annualized cost.

Then, for each tool on the list, define the intended business outcome — the concrete result the tool is supposed to produce. Not the technical functionality. The operational result: time saved, errors reduced, response time improved, revenue activity supported. If leadership cannot define the intended outcome for a tool, that gap is useful information itself. It usually means the tool was adopted reactively, without an explicit purpose, and is a strong candidate for review.

These three steps, inventory, cost, outcome, are the entry point to the AI Business Enablement Audit™. The full audit goes deeper in later chapters. The point here is that the foundation is something a leadership team can begin building today, with data already inside the business.

Before another AI tool is added to the company, do this exercise first. Stop expansion until there is visibility into what already exists. That single act of pausing, looking at the current environment before adding to it, is the moment AI inside the business shifts from reactive accumulation to deliberate management.

Putting It into Practice

The chapter has made the case that unmanaged AI is not a neutral position. It accumulates cost, fragments workflows, degrades output quality, and increases exposure — quietly enough that most leadership teams do not catch the trajectory until something forces them to. The good news is that it is fixable, and the first move is straightforward.

The four steps that follow are designed to be completed within a single week by a leadership team with no AI background. They are the starting point for the full audit framework introduced later in the book.

Step 1 — Build a working AI inventory. Open a spreadsheet. List every AI-related tool currently known to operate inside the business. Including employee-adopted tools, AI features embedded in existing software, and anything leadership personally introduced. Label the document the *AI Tool Inventory*. Treat it as a permanent operational asset, not a one-time exercise.

Step 2 — Reconcile against financial records. Pull credit card statements, recurring software charges, and subscription expenses from the last six months. Flag anything unfamiliar, unreviewed, or quietly auto-renewing. Add each tool to the inventory with its monthly and annual cost. This produces the first defensible picture of total AI spent inside the company.

Step 3 — Assign owners and outcomes. For each tool on the list, define what business outcome it is supposed to produce and who in the company is accountable for that outcome. Ownership should never be vague, "someone in marketing," "the IT team." It should be a person named. If a tool has no clear identifiable purpose or accountable owner, mark it for review during the full audit. Most of the time, those gaps mark exactly the tools that were adopted without intentional planning.

Step 4 — Validate against operational reality. Ask one trusted employee — ideally someone close to day-to-day operations rather than leadership, to complete the inventory exercise independently. Compare the two lists. Any tool that appears on theirs and not on yours is a direct signal of shadow AI inside the business. The objective at this stage is observation, not enforcement. Note the gap. Do not act on it yet.

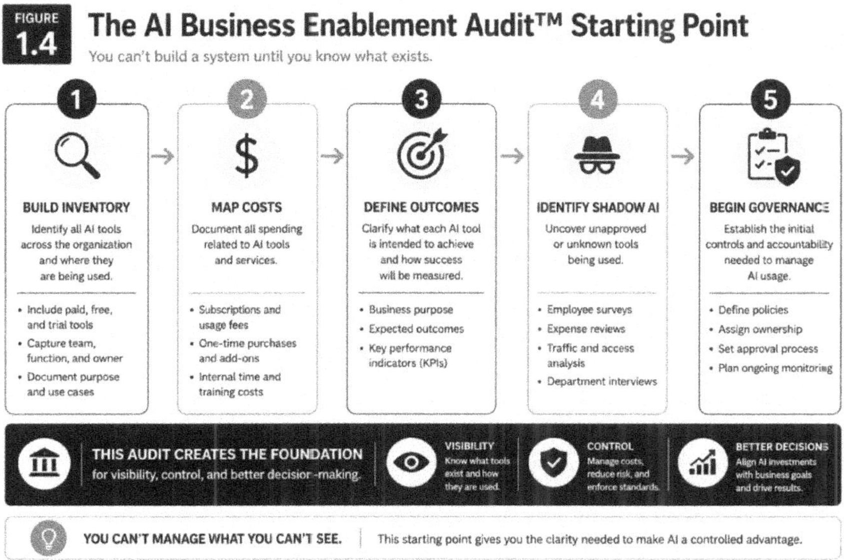

These four steps require no specialized expertise and no budget. They take, in most companies, six to ten hours of work spread over a week. The clarity they produce is the foundation for every other decision the framework introduces. More importantly, they mark the inflection point where AI inside the business stops accumulating reactively and starts operating inside a system.

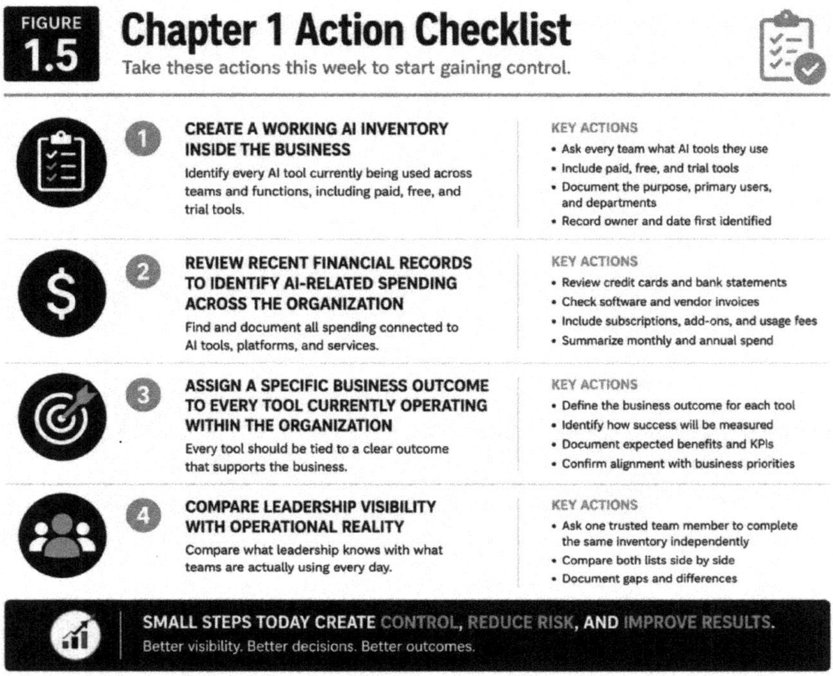
FIGURE 1.5
Chapter 1 Action Checklist
Take these actions this week to start gaining control.
1
CREATE A WORKING AI INVENTORY INSIDE THE BUSINESS
Identify every AI tool currently being used across teams and functions, including paid, free, and trial tools.
KEY ACTIONS
• Ask every team what AI tools they use
• Include paid, free, and trial tools
• Document the purpose, primary users, and departments
• Record owner and date first identified
2
REVIEW RECENT FINANCIAL RECORDS TO IDENTIFY AI-RELATED SPENDING ACROSS THE ORGANIZATION
Find and document all spending connected to AI tools, platforms, and services.
KEY ACTIONS
• Review credit cards and bank statements
• Check software and vendor invoices
• Include subscriptions, add-ons, and usage fees
• Summarize monthly and annual spend
3
ASSIGN A SPECIFIC BUSINESS OUTCOME TO EVERY TOOL CURRENTLY OPERATING WITHIN THE ORGANIZATION
Every tool should be tied to a clear outcome that supports the business.
KEY ACTIONS
• Define the business outcome for each tool
• Identify how success will be measured
• Document expected benefits and KPIs
• Confirm alignment with business priorities
4
COMPARE LEADERSHIP VISIBILITY WITH OPERATIONAL REALITY
Compare what leadership knows with what teams are actually using every day.
KEY ACTIONS
• Ask one trusted team member to complete the same inventory independently
• Compare both lists side by side
• Document gaps and differences
SMALL STEPS TODAY CREATE CONTROL, REDUCE RISK, AND IMPROVE RESULTS.
Better visibility. Better decisions. Better outcomes.

Chapter 2: Shadow AI

The Invisible Risk Already Inside Your Business

CHAPTER OUTCOMES

At the end of this chapter, you will be able to:

- **Define shadow AI** – Understand what shadow AI is, how it spreads, and why it is already operating in your business.
- **Recognize the real risks** – Identify the financial, data privacy, compliance, operational, and reputational risks created by unmanaged AI tools and platforms.
- **Understand the human factor** – See why employees adopt AI tools for good reasons and why the issue is a system gap not an integrity problem.
- **Spot the patterns** – Identify the common ways shadow AI shows up in your organization through tools, features, extensions, and embedded AI.
- **Measure the awareness gap** – Use the gap between leadership awareness and employee disclosure as the first indicator of shadow AI in your business.
- **Protect your data and accountability** – Understand why your company remains responsible for how data is used, even in tools you did not approve.
- **Learn from real-world impact** – See how unapproved AI tools accumulate cost, create exposure, and lead to operational blind spots over time.
- **Commit to visibility and control** – Take the first step toward building a system that makes AI usage visible, governable, and measurable.

What Shadow AI Is and Why It is Already Happening to You

Every audit starts with the same surprise. Leadership names the AI tools they think are in use. The audit names the ones that are. The two lists almost never match, and the second list is almost always longer.

The gap between them has a name: shadow AI.

Shadow AI is any artificial intelligence tool, platform, browser extension, or embedded feature operating inside the business without leadership approval, formal review, or documented oversight. It is not a hypothetical concern. It is a current condition affecting nearly every company worked with, particularly small and mid-sized firms, where technology adoption happens informally and without centralized procurement (Sánchez, Calderón, & Herrera, 2025). The research on organizational AI maturity keeps converging on the same finding: companies struggle with AI less because they cannot find value in technology and more because adoption outruns the governance structures designed to manage it.

The first thing to understand is that shadow AI is not an integrity problem. Employees are not adopting these tools to break rules or expose the company. They are using them because the tools work. A platform that turns a one-hour task into a ten-minute task is a rational decision from the employee's perspective (Kar & Kushwaha, 2021). The problem is not what the employee did. The problem is that the company did not have a system to make that decision visible, governable, or measurable.

Inside a typical business, shadow AI shows up through small operational moves that look inconsequential at the time:

A customer service rep drafts most of her replies in ChatGPT.

Bookkeeper pastes month-end financials into an AI summarizer to get the talking points ready before the partner meeting.

A sales coordinator runs an outbound-email browser extension that rewrites every prospect message before it sends.

A project manager links an AI meeting-notes app to the shared Google Drive so it can scan and summarize team documents.

Each one takes five minutes to set up. Each one feels productive. None of them gets reviewed by anyone before it touches business data.

FIGURE 2.1 **SHADOW AI INSIDE THE BUSINESS**

AI tools are being used across your business—often without your knowledge, approval, or oversight.

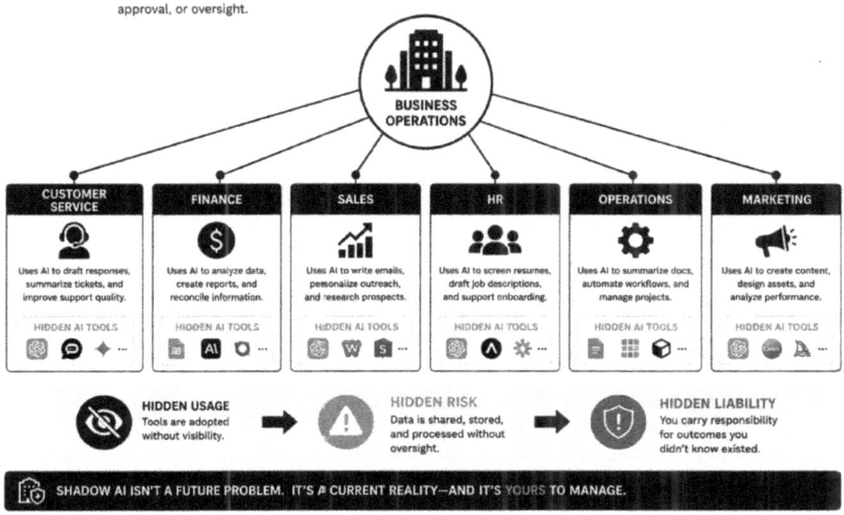

The collective effect is more significant than the individual effect. None of the platforms in those examples show up in IT inventory because they were never procured through IT. Some run on the employee's personal account, paid for with a personal card. Others are buried inside subscriptions the company already pays for, software vendors have been quietly adding AI features through routine updates since late 2023, and most companies have never inventoried what they got. Still others operate as embedded automations: a CRM that now drafts replies, a calendaring tool that now summarizes meetings, an analytics platform that now generates "smart insights." None of it announces itself.

That is what makes shadow AI hard to manage. It does not arrive as a project. It expands through convenience. Because most of the tools are inexpensive or free initially, they do not trigger financial review. Employees discover them, recommend them informally to coworkers, and within a few months a platform is doing real operational work in a part of the business leadership has never thought about.

The exposure is broader than the software inventory. These tools process customer communications, financial documents, internal records, employee information, and proprietary materials. The company is responsible for how that information is managed regardless of whether leadership approved of the tool involved (Sadiq et al., 2021). The absence of visibility does not reduce accountability. In practice, it usually increases it, because risk that no one is managing accumulates faster than risk that is being watched.

FIGURE 2.3 **THE LAYERS OF SHADOW AI**

AI usage in your business exists in multiple layers—most of which remain invisible without deliberate discovery and ongoing visibility.

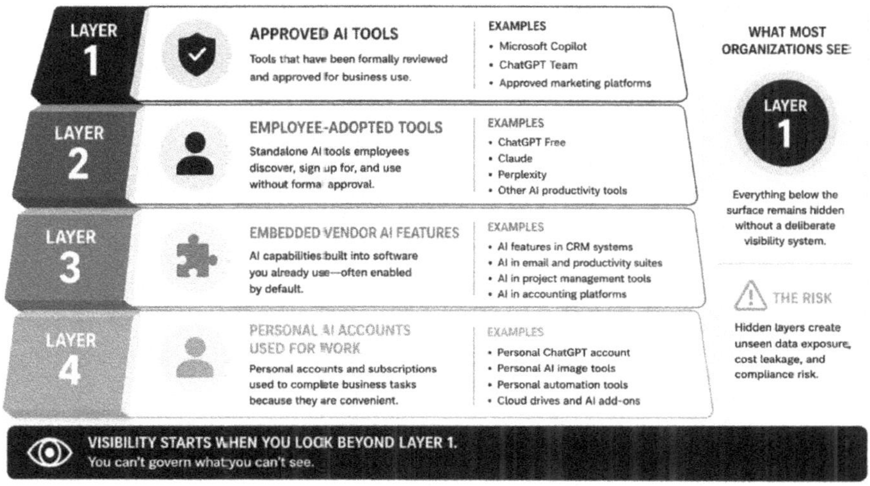

Eventually, unmanaged shadow AI becomes visible the hard way. A client raises concern about an inaccurate output. A compliance review surfaces a vendor relationship leadership did not know existed. A budgeting cycle uncovers six AI subscriptions on three credit cards. At that point, the question is no longer why a specific employee used a specific tool. The question is why the business did not have a system for seeing this coming.

This chapter is about building that system.

Case Example: The Marketing Team That Built an Unapproved AI Stack

A 35-person professional services firm, called Northpoint Advisors, came to me eighteen months ago for a routine operational review. Leadership had a general sense that "the team was using some AI tools" but no clear picture of what or how many. They wanted to know whether they should buy a single enterprise AI subscription to give everyone a shared platform.

When we ran the audit, we found fourteen.

The marketing team had two content-generation platforms. The sales team had an AI-assisted outbound emailer plus a meeting transcription service that quietly ran on every client call. Operations had connected an AI reporting tool to internal spreadsheets to auto-build their monthly leadership update. Three different people had standalone ChatGPT Plus subscriptions on personal accounts they were expensing. Two browser extensions running on company laptops were rewriting customer-facing email drafts. And the finance lead had been using a free online summarizer to digest accounting reports, the same online summarizer whose terms of service included unrestricted rights to use any submitted content for "model improvement."

None of it had been reviewed. Each platform was purchased independently against a department budget. Each subscription looked small in isolation. Together, they accumulated roughly $1,800 per month, nine times what Northpoint's leadership had assumed they were spending on AI in total.

The cost was the easiest part to talk about. The harder findings came up in the second week.

Client deliverables were drifting in tone and quality because each marketing platform produced subtly different languages, and no one was reviewing output for consistency. Two sales reps had been using the meeting transcription service on calls with regulated-industry clients whose contracts explicitly prohibited third-party recording. The reporting tool connected to operations had read-write access to financial spreadsheets it did not need, a permissions issue no one had configured deliberately. And the finance lead's "free summarizer" had, over the prior nine months, ingested most of the firm's monthly P&Ls.

The fix was structural rather than punitive. We consolidated the marketing tools to a single approved platform. We replaced the meeting transcription service with an enterprise-grade equivalent the firm could vet contractually. We retired the free summarizer, audited what data had been submitted to it, and built an internal review checklist for finance summaries. We wrote a one-page AI usage policy and stood up a fifteen-minute monthly review.

Within six months, Northpoint had cut AI subscription costs by 40%, eliminated three meaningful compliance exposures, and had, for the first time, an accurate inventory of every AI tool operating inside the company. Adoption did not slow. If anything, it accelerated, because employees now had clear approved channels for adding new tools rather than working around them.

The pattern is not unusual. It is the pattern.

FIGURE 2.4 HOW TO SURFACE SHADOW AI WITHOUT CREATING DISTRUST

Your approach determines whether employees hide AI usage—or help you manage it.

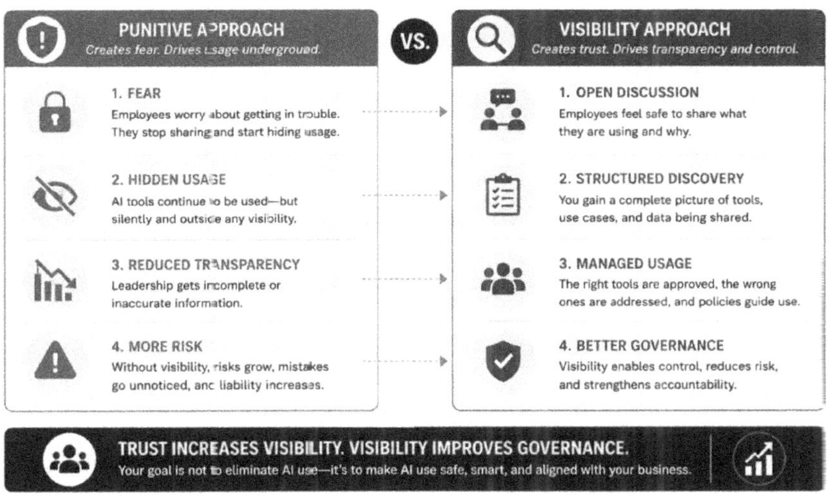

The Real Liability Behind Unauthorized AI Usage

When an employee pastes sensitive business information into an unapproved AI tool, the liability that follows does not stay with the employee. It rests with the company.

That is true regardless of intent. Confidentiality agreements, client contracts, privacy obligations, and industry compliance requirements bind the organization, not the individual user (Pumplun, Tauchert, & Heidt, 2019). If a regulator or a client wants to know how their data was handled, the company has to answer, and the answer "an employee did it without our approval" does not separate the business from the consequences. In many cases, the absence of formal oversight makes the situation worse, because the company cannot demonstrate that reasonable controls were in place.

This is where a governance concept worth knowing comes in: *data provenance*. Data provenance is the ability to trace where operational data originated, how it has moved between systems, and whether the external platforms processing it are doing so under terms the company agreed to. When unmanaged AI tools sit in the workflow, that chain breaks. The company loses the ability to say with confidence where its data has been, who has had access to it, or what was done with it after it left internal systems.

Consider a scenario that gets less hypothetical every quarter:

An operations manager at a healthcare services company is preparing for a leadership meeting. She has thirty minutes and a four-page patient intake summary to digest into talking points. She finds a free online AI summarizer through a Google search, pastes the document in, and gets back exactly what she needed in under a minute. Operationally, the move makes sense. From a regulatory standpoint, she has just transmitted protected health information to a third-party platform the company has no agreement with, no business associate agreement with, and no visibility into.

Six months later, the company undergoes a routine compliance audit. The audit asks what third-party services have processed patient data over the prior year. No one can answer cleanly. The summarizer was never inventoried because it was free. The vendor's terms of service, which no one ever read, asserts the right to retain submitted content and use it to train future models.

The intent was harmless. The exposure is not.

Healthcare is the cleanest example because regulatory obligations are well defined, but the same dynamic appears in every industry that handles confidential information:

- Legal firms — privileged client communications and case files.
- Accounting and financial advisory — tax returns, banking details, financial statements.

- Real estate — contracts, ID documents, transaction records.
- Professional services generally — proprietary client information governed by NDAs and master services agreements.

Wherever the business has agreed to manage information a certain way, unauthorized AI usage opens a gap between what the contract says and what is happening operationally.

The liability extends beyond data handling. AI tools increasingly influence decisions, not just process information. They draft customer-facing emails. They generate hiring recommendations. They produce financial summaries that inform pricing. They flag patterns that shape operational priorities. The company stays accountable for those decisions regardless of how they were generated the AI vendor does not absorb the responsibility just because their software produced the output (Yablonsky, 2021). Without a governance layer that requires explainability, review, and assigned ownership for consequential outputs, leadership ends up answering for decisions the company cannot fully reconstruct.

There is also a financial dimension that gets overlooked. Free AI tools are rarely free in the meaningful sense. The vendor's business model is usually data, model training rights, advertising data, broad usage rights tucked into the terms of service. When employees feed business information into those platforms, the company may not be paying with money, but it is paying with operational data: client details, pricing structures, internal workflows, strategic plans. The exchange is real, even when no invoice ever lands.

None of this is meant to provoke alarm. The point is the opposite. Once the shape of the exposure is visible, it becomes manageable. Businesses cannot govern what they cannot see. The rest of this chapter is about how to surface what is happening, without making employees afraid to tell you.

How to Surface Shadow AI Without Creating a Culture of Distrust

The first instinct, when leadership realizes how much shadow AI is in the building, is to lock things down. Block tools. Require approval for everything. Send a stern email about unauthorized software.

It is the wrong instinct.

The research is consistent on this point, when shadow IT discovery is run as an enforcement campaign, transparency collapses (Dey et al., 2023). Tools do not disappear because leadership disapproves of them. Usage just goes underground. Employees become less willing to tell management what they are doing, and the company ends up with the worst possible outcome: continued usage with reduced visibility. The exposure stays. The ability to manage it shrinks.

The companies that bring shadow AI under control quickly do it differently. They treat the first phase as a listening exercise, not a compliance audit. Employees are using these tools because they solve real problems — a slow approval cycle, repetitive task, a workflow no one ever fixed. That information is operationally useful. Before any governance structure can be built, leadership needs an honest picture of where AI has filled a gap the business had not addressed.

That changes how the first conversation should go.

Lead with the framing explicitly. The company is building a formal AI management system, and to do that it needs to see what is happening today. The discovery is not disciplinary. The point is not to find policy violations — there are no policies yet to violate. The point is to understand the current operational reality so the company can manage it intentionally.

A few questions work well in that first conversation:

- What AI tools, assistants, browser extensions, or automated platforms are you currently using for work-related tasks?

- What specific tasks are they helping you with?

- What kinds of company, customer, or operational information do you enter them?

Document everything. Do not react. Do not promise that any specific tool will or will not be allowed. The goal of the first pass is visibility, not adjudication.

FIGURE 2.5 **THE SHADOW AI AUDIT PROCESS**

A repeatable seven-step process to uncover, assess, and manage shadow AI risk across your business.

Most owners are surprised by what comes up. Tools of which they have never heard. Workflows that have been entirely re-engineered around an AI assistant. Inventive use cases that have produced real productivity gains nobody told leadership about. They are also sometimes surprised by what kind of data has been moving through unvetted platforms. Whatever surfaces, the most important leadership discipline at this stage is staying measured. Disclosure plus calm response is what builds the trust the rest of the framework depends on.

After the conversational pass, do a light technical review to fill in the gaps. This does not require surveillance software or aggressive monitoring. It is the same review a serious IT manager already does once a year:

Look at connected applications in Google Workspace, Microsoft 365, your CRM, and shared file environments. Most of these platforms expose "Apps with access to your account" inside admin settings.

Inventory browser extensions on company-managed devices.

Pull a quarter of credit-card statements and flag every recurring software charge against the inventory the team produced in the conversational pass.

The technical sweep always uncovers tools the employee conversations missed, embedded integrations, dormant subscriptions, AI features inside platforms employees do not even recognize as AI. Together with the employee disclosures, the result is the most complete operational picture the business has ever had of what AI is doing inside it.

A final discipline matters do not make examples of the people who disclose unauthorized usage. The whole framework depends on transparency. If the first employee who tells you about a tool gets disciplined, no one will tell you about the second tool, the third tool, or the new one that shows up next month. Some tools will turn out to be perfectly fine and worth formalizing. Others will need to be replaced or retired. Both outcomes are manageable. What is not manageable is a workforce that has learned to hide what it is using.

Shadow AI is, at root, a culture problem before it is a governance problem. The companies that solve it well solve it by building enough trust that employees keep surfacing reality, while leadership builds the structure to manage the reality once it is visible.

Building Your First AI Visibility Layer

Once shadow AI has been surfaced, the work shifts from discovery to maintenance. Discovery is a moment. Visibility is a habit.

The AI Visibility Layer is the system that turns the one-time discovery into an ongoing operating discipline. It is not complicated, and it does not require any innovative technology. Three components, each lightweight:

- A centralized AI tool inventory.
- A short approval process for new AI tools.
- A recurring monthly review.

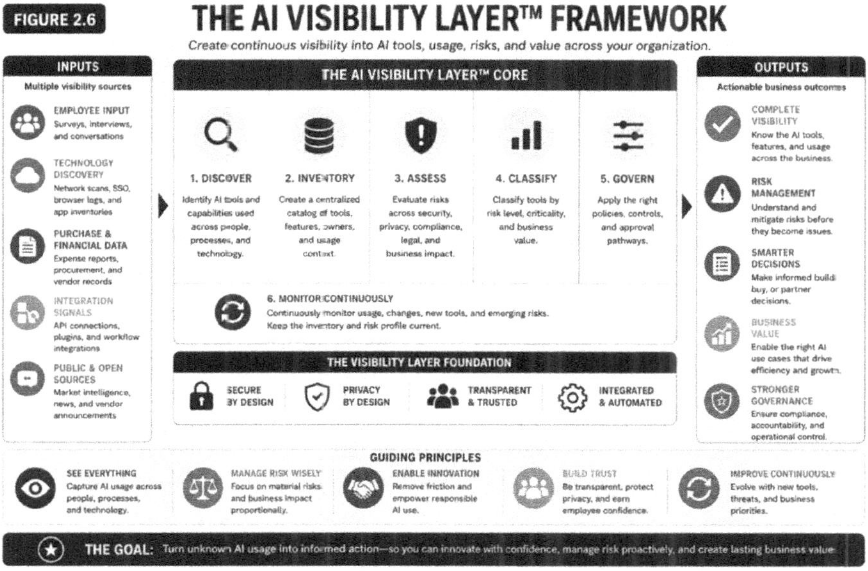

FIGURE 2.6

Most companies can stand up all three in a single afternoon. The clarity they create is the foundation that every later component of the framework depends on.

The inventory. Open a shared spreadsheet or database. For every AI-related tool currently operating inside the business, capture: tool name, primary function, the department, or person using it, the type of data it processes, monthly and annual cost, approval status, and date it was introduced into operations. The inventory should include far more than the leadership tools formally approved. It should include everything surfaced during the discovery conversations: employee-found tools, browser extensions, embedded AI features inside existing software, and any external services touching company data.

Expect gaps. The first time through, leadership often does not know precisely what data certain tools process, where that data is stored, or whether the vendor retains it for model training. Those gaps are themselves useful, they mark exactly the tools that need a closer review. For each one, pull the vendor's privacy policy, terms of service, and security documentation. Pay particular attention to data storage, retention, model training rights, third-party sharing, and administrative controls. If a vendor cannot answer those questions clearly, that is itself a finding.

Figure 2.7 — Shadow AI Control Cycle™

A Continuous Cycle for Visibility, Governance, and Operational Control

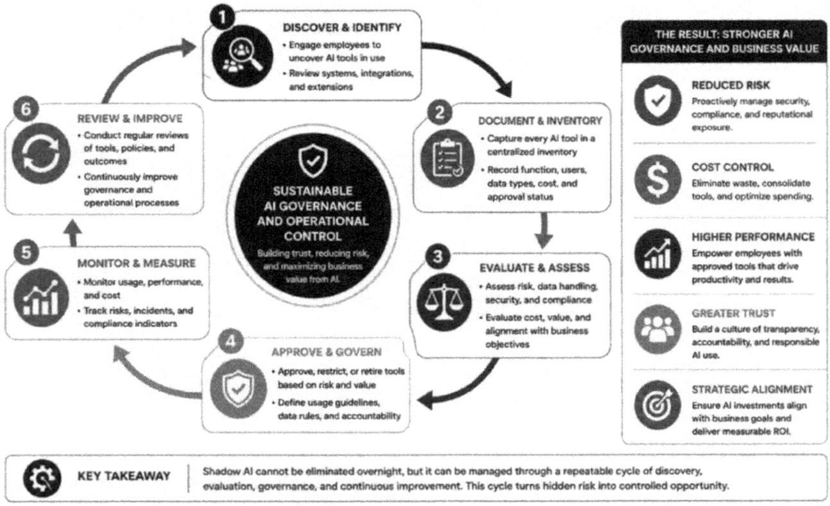

The approval process. Going forward, no new AI tool enters the business until it has been documented in the inventory and runs through a four-question review. The questions are operational, not bureaucratic:

- What specific problem does this tool solve?
- What kind of business or customer data will it process?
- What does it cost — fully loaded, including usage-based growth?
- Do we already have an approved tool that does the same thing?

In a well-run company, the review takes fifteen minutes. The point is not to slow adoption. The point is to make sure adoption decisions are deliberate, documented, and visible to leadership before the company is dependent on the tool.

The monthly review. Visibility built once is visibility lost over time. The fix is a recurring fifteen-minute checkpoint, call it the AI Inventory Review, with whoever owns operations, technology, or governance in the company. The agenda is three questions:

- Have any new AI tools shown up since last month that are not yet in inventory?

- Are any tools on the inventory no longer being used and worth retiring?
- Have any costs, integrations, or usage patterns shifted materially?

That is the whole meeting. Done consistently, it is what keeps the company from drifting back into pre-audit condition.

How leadership communicates the visibility layer matters as much as its mechanics. If employees experience it as monitoring, transparency drops and so does the inventory's accuracy. If they experience it as support, a way to avoid paying for duplicate tools, a way to surface what is already working, a way to make sure no one accidentally puts client data somewhere that creates exposure — the inventory grows organically. Both framings produce the same spreadsheet on day one. Only one of them keeps producing accurate data on day ninety.

The Visibility Layer will not catch every tool on the first pass. New tools will keep entering the business. Some employees will keep experimenting. That is fine. The objective is not perfect control on day one. The objective is a repeatable process that keeps AI usage visible, intentional, and manageable, and that grows in coverage every month rather than degrading.

Research on AI adoption maturity has documented the difference this kind of structure makes. Companies that implement integrated governance and adoption frameworks, workforce enablement plus operational integration plus active leadership oversight, report AI initiative success rates as high as 74%. Companies operating without that structure report success rates as low as 12%. Technology is the same. The management discipline around it is not.

Your Next Move

Shadow AI is not a future governance problem. It is a present operating condition in nearly every company, with between twenty and a thousand employees. Exposure exists whether the business acknowledges it or not. The purpose of this chapter has been to make the condition visible and to hand over the tools to bring it under control.

The work that follows is execution.

Within the next five business days, schedule the discovery conversation with the team. Use the three questions from earlier in this chapter. Document everything. Do not react in the room. The goal of the conversation is visibility, not enforcement.

Within the next two weeks, stand up the first version of the AI Visibility Layer inventory. Tool name, function, owner, data, cost, approval status, date introduced. Include everything that came up in the discovery, everything leadership already knew about, and everything the technical sweep uncovers. Expect to find more than you thought it was there.

Figure 2.8 — Structured AI Governance Success Gap™

Comparing Operational Outcomes With and Without Structured AI Governance

Within the next thirty days, put the monthly AI Inventory Review on the calendar and run it once. Fifteen minutes. The three questions above. After the second or third month, the meeting becomes self-sustaining, leadership knows what to look for, employees know what to bring, and the inventory stays current with much less effort than it took to build.

None of this requires consultants, technical expertise, or significant budget. It requires the same operating discipline you already bring to functions that are taken more seriously. The choice in front of the business is not whether to use AI. AI is already operating inside the company. The choice is whether that usage stays fragmented and reactive — or whether it becomes visible, structured, and intentionally managed.

That distinction defines the difference between companies that have AI tools and companies that have AI infrastructure. The next chapter is about turning the visibility built here into a full diagnostic, the AI Business Enablement Audit™.

Chapter 3: The AI Business Enablement Audit™

Your Starting Point for Everything

CHAPTER OUTCOMES

At the end of this chapter, you will be able to:

Explain what the AI Business Enablement Audit™ is
and why it is the essential starting point for managing AI in your business.

Understand the five audit dimensions
tool inventory, cost mapping, performance measurement, risk exposure, and governance gaps—and the question each dimension answers.

Build a complete operational picture
of how AI is operating in your business across tools, spending, performance, risk, and governance.

Identify what is working, what is not, and why
separating tools that deliver measurable value from those that are idle, redundant, or underperforming.

Assess risk and exposure
identify where sensitive data, decisions, vendors, and compliance are most at risk.

Uncover governance gaps
identify missing policies, processes, ownership, and controls that must be established.

Establish a defensible baseline
create the benchmarks and documentation that every future AI decision and review will be measured against.

Run the audit efficiently
complete the audit in 8–12 hours over two weeks without disrupting daily operations.

Produce the four core audit artifacts
tool inventory, cost & performance baseline, risk map, and governance gap list.

Use audit insights to drive action
turn findings into cost savings, risk reduction, and measurable business impact.

The audit gives you clarity. Clarity gives you control. **Control creates value.** This is the foundation of The AI Operating System™.

What the Audit Is and Why It Comes Before Everything Else

By now the diagnosis is no longer abstract. AI is operating inside the business through tools nobody fully tracks, costing more than anyone estimated, producing outputs nobody is measuring, and introducing risk nobody has named. The previous chapters built visibility into that condition. Visibility is the prerequisite. It is not the destination.

The destination is a structured, repeatable management system. The transition from one to the other begins with the AI Business Enablement Audit™, the diagnostic engine at the center of The AI Operating System™.

The audit produces a documented, current, defensible picture of how AI is operating inside the company today. Not what leadership remembers approving. Not what employees informally report. Not what the budget shows. What is happening across every function, every team, every dollar. Until that picture exists, every decision about AI is built on partial information (Jöhnk et al., 2020), and the cost of those decisions compounds over time.

The logic is the same as every other serious operational diagnostic. No one would redesign a sales process without first mapping how it currently runs. No one would restructure a team without an accurate view of who does what. No one would renegotiate vendor contracts without understanding what is being paid and what is being delivered. The audit applies that same discipline to AI, a category of spend, risk, and operational influence that has, in most businesses, never received it.

The audit is built around **five dimensions: tool inventory, cost mapping, performance measurement, risk exposure, and governance gaps** (Kalleparambil & Akoum, 2025). Each dimension answers one specific question and produces one specific output. Together they form a complete operational picture of how AI functions inside the business, and a working baseline that every later decision is measured against.

This is not a consulting engagement. It does not require outside resources, advanced technical capability, or a multi-month project plan. It is an operator-level review designed to fit inside the rhythm of a normal business, eight to twelve hours of leadership time over a two-week window. When running well, it produces the most valuable artifact the business has ever had for managing AI: a clear view of reality.

The Five Audit Dimensions Every Business Must Evaluate

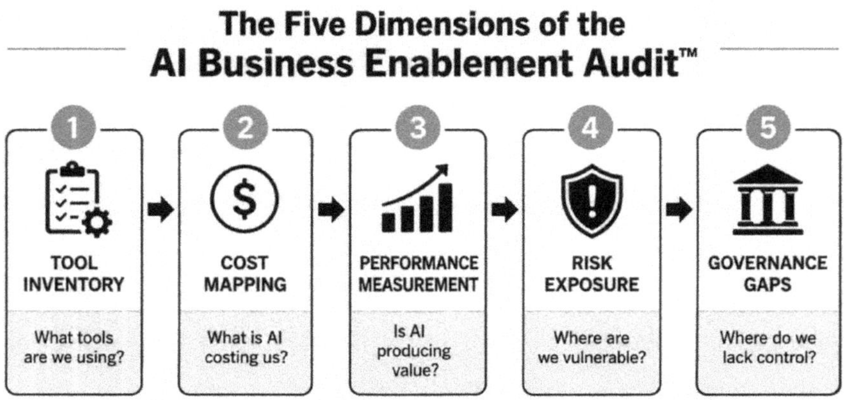

Figure 3.1: The Five Dimensions of the AI Business Enablement Audit™

Each dimension asks a simple question. The questions sound easy. The answers never are. That gap between what the questions appear to require and what the business has documented, is where most of the cost, risk, and missed value hides.

Dimension One — Tool Inventory. What AI tools are we actually using? Not the ones leadership remembers approving. Everyone, employee-adopted platforms, embedded AI features inside existing software, browser extensions, personal accounts being used for company work, AI capabilities the vendor turned on through an update last quarter. The output of this dimension is a documented inventory with consistent data for every tool in the environment.

Dimension Two — Cost Mapping. What is AI costing us? Subscription fees are the easy answer. The harder picture includes usage-based charges that grow with adoption, tier upgrades made without review, premium features added quietly to existing contracts, and the labor cost of operating, validating, and correcting AI outputs. The output is a full cost map, always significantly larger than the pre-audit estimate.

Dimension Three — Performance Measurement. Are these tools producing measurable business value? Each tool gets tied to a defined outcome, time saved, errors reduced, revenue supported, response times improved, and evaluated against evidence rather than impression. The output is a performance baseline that separates tools delivering value from tools running on inertia.

Dimension Four — Risk Exposure. Where is the business vulnerable? Risk in this category covers data exposure (what information is leaving the company through these tools), decision exposure (where AI outputs influence business decisions without review), vendor dependency, and compliance alignment. The output is a documented risk map with the highest exposures flagged.

Dimension Five — Governance Gaps. Where do we lack control? This dimension surfaces the management infrastructure that does not yet exist missing policies, non-existent approval processes, undefined ownership, absent review standards. The output is a prioritized list of governance work that becomes the basis for the next sixty to ninety days.

Each dimension feeds the next. Inventory shapes the cost map. Cost and performance together identify what is worth measuring more closely. Risk concentrates on the governance work. The five dimensions are not five independent assessments, they are five layers of one operational picture, and that picture only becomes useful when all five exist together. Research on AI maturity has been consistent on this point: organizations that evaluate only the technology layer while neglecting accountability, leadership alignment, and governance processes account for the majority of AI initiatives that fail to produce measurable value.

How to Run the Audit Without Disrupting Operations

The word audit usually triggers resistance. Most owners associate it with weeks of disruption, stacks of documentation, and a report no one reads. That is not what this audit is. The AI Business Enablement Audit™ is designed to be run by an operating team during normal business hours, in eight to twelve total hours of leadership time spread across two weeks.

The process has three phases.

Phase 1 — Data Collection (Days 1–3). Build the tool inventory and complete the cost map. Pull credit card statements, recurring software charges, and accounting records for the previous six months. Capture every AI-related platform — approved, employee-adopted, embedded, or unclear. When in doubt, include it; pruning happens later.

Phase 2 — Analysis (Days 4–9). Evaluate performance and risk. For each tool, define the intended business outcome and assess whether it is being delivered. For each tool, review what data it touches, what vendor terms cover that data, and what dependency it has created. Flag the high-risk items for the governance phase that follows.

Phase 3 — Synthesis (Days 10–14). Identify governance gaps. Review where policies, approval processes, and review mechanisms are absent or inconsistent. Consolidate the findings into the four audit outputs (inventory, cost and performance baseline, risk map, governance gap list). A focused two-hour synthesis session is usually enough to complete this step.

Role definition is what keeps the audit efficient. One person, typically who owns operations or finance, leads data collection and consolidation. A brief team conversation gathers input from people closer to specific workflows. Beyond that, most of the work happens without interrupting day-to-day operations. The audit is meant to inform the business, not slow it.

Dimension One — Building a Complete Tool Inventory

The inventory is the foundation. Every other dimension depends on it being complete. A partial inventory produces a partial cost picture, a partial performance picture, and a partial risk picture — and decisions made against those are partial decisions (Uren & Edwards, 2023).

Start with the working inventory you began in the previous chapter and treat it as a draft, not a finished list. Expand, validate, and structure it. The discipline at this stage is completeness, not speed.

Each tool gets documented against a standard set of fields: Tool name. One-sentence description of what it does.

1. Owner — the named person or team responsible.

2. Data handled — what kind of company, customer, or operational information moves through it.

3. Monthly cost — fully loaded, including usage-based charges.

4. Approval status — formally approved, informally adopted, or unclear.

5. Date introduced — when the tool started operating inside the business.

Tool Name	Description	Owner	Data Handled	Monthly Cost	Approval Status	Usage
Example Tool	AI writing assistant	Marketing	Client text	$49	Informal	Active

Figure 3.2 — AI Tool Inventory: sample row

Gaps in the inventory are not minor. They are signals of missing visibility, and they will distort every downstream decision. If a field is empty, fill it. Check the vendor's privacy policy for data-handling questions. Check the billing record for cost questions. Identify the actual user for ownership questions. The fields are simple. The discipline of completing them is what turns a list into a working management document.

Once the core fields are filled in, classify each tool by current usage: *active*, *marginal*, or *idle*. Active tools are used consistently and play a defined role. Marginal tools are used inconsistently or without evaluation. Idle tools are still being paid for but barely used. Most first-time audits find a meaningful share of the inventory falls into the idle and marginal categories that is the predictable result of decentralized adoption, and it is the easiest money the audit will surface (Sadiq et al., 2021) .

Completing this inventory is the moment the business stops guessing about its own AI usage and starts managing it. Every later dimension assumes this artifact exists.

Dimension Two — Mapping What AI Is Actually Costing You

AI spend rarely arrives as one large invoice. It accumulates across subscriptions, seat additions, premium tier upgrades, usage-based overages, consulting fees, and embedded vendor enhancements that scale gradually over time. The result is a category of spend that is always larger than the pre-audit estimate, typically thirty to fifty percent higher, and sometimes more (Poon et al., 2025).

For each tool on the inventory, capture the true monthly cost: base subscription, seat licenses, usage charges, premium features, and any add-ons. Where charges fluctuate, they average them across multiple months. The objective is a defensible monthly number, not a point-in-time snapshot.

Category	Monthly Cost	Annual Cost
Content tools	$300	$3,600
Automation tools	$250	$3,000
Analytics tools	$400	$4,800
Total	**$950**	**$11,400**

Figure 3.3 — AI Cost Map: sample category rollup

Figure 3.3 — AI Cost Map: sample category rollup

Costs that never show up in accounting matters too. Every AI tool carries some operational overhead, the time spent learning it, reviewing its outputs, switching between platforms, fixing what it got wrong. None of that appears on a P&L. All of it shows up in throughput. A tool that saves twenty hours and costs fifteen in review work is producing net value of five hours, not twenty.

Once the full cost map is built, patterns surface that were invisible before. Multiple tools pay for the same capability. Subscriptions that have not been used in months. Pricing that scaled with usage in ways nobody flagged. These patterns are predictable. They are also where the first round of cost savings always comes from.

Cost mapping does not exist to cut spending. It exists to make spending visible. With a baseline in place, every later decision, a new subscription, a tier upgrade, a vendor switch, gets evaluated against documented numbers rather than estimates. That is what turns AI from an uncontrolled expense into a managed investment.

Dimension Three — Measuring What AI Is Actually Producing

The hardest question in the audit is the one most companies avoid. Are these tools producing measurable value, or do they just feel useful? Productivity feels improved. Tasks feel faster. The actual delta is rarely measured.

Performance measurement starts with outcomes, not features. Every tool gets tied to a specific business result expressed in the language the business already uses time saved, errors reduced, revenue activity supported, customer response time improved, compliance work accelerated. If a tool cannot be tied to a defined outcome, that is itself a finding, the tool was probably adopted without a clear purpose and is worth a closer look (Soomro et al., 2025).

Tool	Expected Outcome	Time Saved	Output Quality	ROI Score
Example Tool	Faster content creation	High	Medium	4 / 5

Figure 3.4 — AI Performance Scorecard: sample row

Evidence does not have to be precise to be useful. A reasonable estimate, applied consistently across tools, is more valuable than an exhaustive measurement of one tool and silence about the rest. If a writing assistant cuts a typical draft from forty-five minutes to fifteen, that is the number. Validate it across two or three users to make sure it generalizes. Move on.

Performance is not static. A tool that works well today may degrade as workloads change, as employees grow past it, or as vendor updates shift its behavior. The opposite happens too — a tool that felt marginal at adoption may become essential as workflows evolve around it. The performance picture has to be revisited.

When performance gets measured, three things become visible. The tools that justify their cost. The tools that look productive but are creating compensatory work elsewhere. And the tools that nobody can defend in concrete terms. The first category gets protected. The second gets fixed. The third becomes a candidate for retirement at the next budget review.

Dimension Four — Assessing Your Risk Exposure

AI risk does not look like traditional operational risk. It is embedded inside tools that appear to improve productivity, which makes it easy to miss. A platform that saves four hours of work may also be retaining sensitive data on external servers, influencing decisions without review, or quietly creating a dependency the business cannot easily unwind. The audit makes that exposure visible.

Mature risk evaluation runs across the full lifecycle of each tool, at adoption, during active operation, and as workflows and vendor practices change over time. Evaluating risk only at the moment a tool is approved misses the largest category of exposure, which is drift: usage growing, dependencies deepening, terms of service changing under the contract without anyone noticing.

Four categories of risk are worth surfacing explicitly:

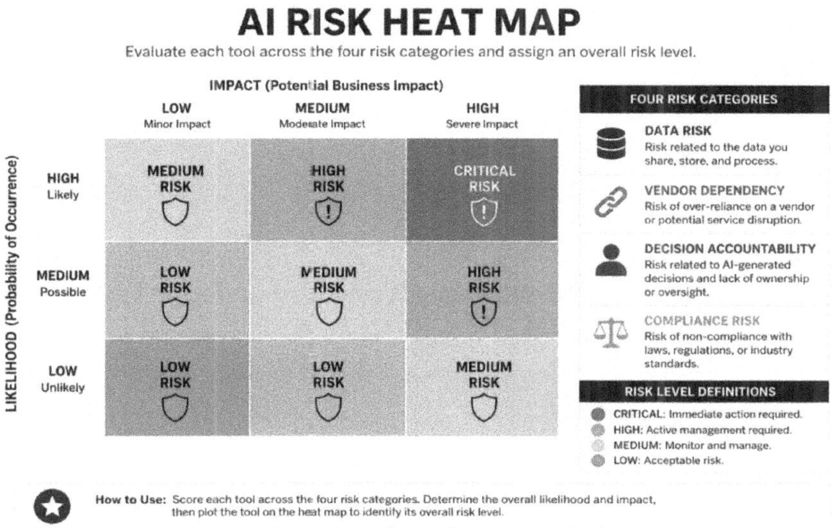

Figure 3.5 — AI Risk Heat Map

Data exposure. What information is the tool processing, where does it go, how is it stored, and what rights has the vendor reserved? Review the privacy policy and terms of service for every tool that touches customer, financial, or otherwise sensitive data (Pumplun et al., 2019). A vendor that cannot answer those questions cleanly is itself a finding.

Decision accountability. Where do AI output influence consequential business decisions — pricing, hiring, customer-facing communications, financial reporting? Each of those decisions still rests with the company. Without a named human owner and a defined review step, the business is absorbing accountability for outputs it cannot reconstruct.

Vendor dependency. Which workflows have become reliant on a specific platform? What happens if pricing changes, terms shift, or the vendor discontinues a feature? Dependency forms quietly; the cost of unwinding it does not.

Compliance alignment. Particularly relevant in regulated industries, but never zero. Where is the business making contractual or regulatory commitments about how data is handled, and do those commitments hold up against how AI tools are using the data today?

The objective is not to eliminate risk. The objective is to make it visible, prioritized, and managed. Most audits find that risk is concentrated in a handful of tools and processes, usually those touching the most sensitive data or the most consequential decisions. That concentration is helpful. It tells the company where to focus on the governance work that follows.

Dimension Five — Identifying Your Governance Gaps

The final dimension addresses the question that connects everything else: where do we lack control? At this point in the audit the company knows what tools exist, what they cost, how they perform, and where they expose the business. What remains is whether there are structures in place to manage any of it. In most companies, this is where the gaps are widest.

Governance does not require complexity. It requires clarity, about who decides, who reviews, who owns, and what standards apply. Without it, AI usage is driven by individual choice rather than organizational direction. The output of this dimension is a prioritized list of the governance work the business needs to do.

Governance Element	Status		
AI usage policy exists	☐ Yes	☐ No	☐ Partial
Tool approval process exists	☐ Yes	☐ No	☐ Partial
Data handling rules documented	☐ Yes	☐ No	☐ Partial
Output review process defined	☐ Yes	☐ No	☐ Partial
Ownership assigned for every tool	☐ Yes	☐ No	☐ Partial

Figure 3.6 — Governance gap checklist

Walk through the checklist function by function — client communications, internal reporting, hiring, finance, customer service. For each area, the question is whether the standard exists, whether it is documented, and whether anyone in the business could follow it without leadership translation. Verbal norms do not count. If it is not written down, it is not a governance control.

Most businesses find at first audit that the checklist is mostly empty. That is not a failure. It is the predictable consequence of technology adoption that outran management. The valuable outcome is that the gaps are now visible. With visibility, the company can prioritize the governance work by impact and urgency rather than trying to build everything at once.

The audit is now complete across all five dimensions. The company has visibility in its tools, clarity on cost, evidence on performance, awareness of risk, and a documented list of governance gaps. Together these elements form the first complete picture the business has ever had of how AI operates inside it.

What You'll Have When the Audit Is Complete

The audit produces four working artifacts. They are not reports that get filed and forgotten. They are operating documents that get used, updated, and referenced going forward.

Figure 3.7 — The Four Audit Outputs™

The AI Tool Inventory. Every tool operating inside the business, documented against a consistent set of fields. The single source of truth for AI usage.

The Cost and Performance Baseline. Total AI spend, broken out by tool and category, tied to defined business outcomes. The reference point against which every future AI investment is evaluated.

The Risk Map. Documented exposure across data handling, decision accountability, vendor dependency, and compliance alignment. The basis for what needs governance attention first.

The Governance Gap List. A prioritized list of the policies, processes, and ownership structures the business needs to build. Becomes the action plan for the next sixty to ninety days.

Together, these four artifacts represent a material shift in how AI operates inside the company. What was fragmented becomes documented. What was reactive becomes deliberate. What was guessed becomes measured. That shift is what allows the rest of the framework — cost control, performance management, governance, operational integration, to be built on something other than estimates (Westover, 2025).

Finishing the audit is not the end of anything. It is the start of running AI as a managed function rather than discovering it as a surprise.

Preparing Your Team for the Audit Process

The audit requires input from the team, and how leadership frames the request determines how useful the responses are. Positioned as a compliance exercise, the audit produces minimal information and a lot of caution. Positioned to make the team's tools safer, more effective, and less duplicative, the same audit produces candid information.

The framing is direct. The business is building a structured AI management system and needs an honest picture of current usage to do it. The goal is not to find policy violations; no policies exist yet. The goal is to make sure the tools people are using are supported, safe, and worth keeping.

Pick a small set of people to provide input rather than blanketing the company. Typically: someone in operations, someone client-facing, someone responsible for finance or technology. Each gets a clear, narrow ask, what AI tools are you using, what tasks do they support, what information do you put into them, and a defined format that makes consolidation easy. A five-business-day deadline keeps momentum without creating pressure to skim.

When responses come back, the discipline stays neutral. Do not react to surprising disclosures in the moment. Document them. If a specific tool needs immediate attention, handle it privately after the audit is completed. Visible reactions during the discovery phase produce predictable results: less disclosure on the next round.

Set the expectation that the audit is not a one-time event. A lighter version of the same review happens on a recurring cadence going forward. The first audit takes the most effort because it builds the artifacts from scratch. Every subsequent cycle is faster because the structure is already in place. Over time, the audit becomes part of how the business operates rather than a project the business runs.

Your Audit Quick-Start Sequence

The work below is the operating version of the audit, a day-by-day sequence designed to be followed exactly. Move deliberately. Each day's work feeds the next.

Figure 3.8 — Two-Week Audit Timeline

Day 1. Open the working inventory from the previous chapter. Confirm every required field — name, description, owner, data, cost, approval status, date introduced. Fill in what you know. Mark gaps.

Day 2. Reconcile cost. Pull out credit card statements, recurring software charges, and accounting records for the last six months. Add every AI-related charge to the inventory. Calculate monthly and annual totals. Capture the baseline number in a visible place.

Day 3. Send the team request. Targeted ask to the three or four people you identified, with the standard format and a five-day deadline. While waiting, begin defining intended outcomes for every active tool already on the inventory.

Days 4–7. Risk assessment. For every tool, evaluate data exposure, vendor dependency, decision accountability, and compliance alignment. Assign a risk level. Flag high-risk items for the governance phase.

Days 8–14. Consolidate. Integrate team responses into the inventory. Close remaining gaps. Run the governance gap checklist function by function. Prioritize. Hold a two-hour synthesis session to finalize the four audit outputs.

When the two weeks are done, the business has a documented, current, defensible picture of how AI is operating across its operations, and a prioritized action plan for what to do next. That is the entire purpose of the audit. Everything that follows in this book is built on it.

When the two weeks are done, the business has a documented, current, defensible picture of how AI is operating across its operations, and a prioritized action plan for what to do next. That is the entire purpose of the audit. Everything that follows in this book is built on it.

Chapter 4: Building Your AI Tool Inventory

Know Exactly What You're Running

CHAPTER OUTCOMES

At the end of this chapter, you will be able to:

Explain why most businesses underestimate their AI usage – Understand how AI is embedded in existing software, features, automations, and employee-adopted tools.

Apply the AI Tool Inventory Framework – Capture every AI-related tool using the six standardized fields: name, function, owner, monthly cost, contract terms, and performance.

Identify true ownership and usage – Name owners, understand who is using each tool, and differentiate between active, idle, and redundant usage.

Calculate total AI spend accurately – Capture fully loaded monthly costs, including variable usage, tiers, and hidden charges.

Document contract terms and renewal risk – Track renewal dates, cancellation notice requirements, and pricing escalations to avoid surprises and unmanaged renewals.

Establish performance baseline – Record the current status of each tool (active, idle, trial, redundant, or unknown) and any known value delivered.

Identify risk and data exposure – Document what data each tool processes, where it is stored, and the level of business risk.

Create a living inventory you can trust – Build a centralized, accurate inventory that becomes the visibility foundation for cost control, risk management, and performance.

You can't manage what you don't know. A complete, accurate inventory is the foundation for every decision that follows.

Why Most Businesses Don't Know What They're Actually Using

Ask an owner what AI tools are operating inside the company and the answer usually comes quickly. ChatGPT. The CRM's predictive features. A writing assistant a department lead recommended a few months back. Maybe an automation platform someone in operations set up. The answer sounds confident because the tools that come to mind first are the ones personally approved or personally uses leadership.

Those are the visible layers. They are rarely the full picture.

When companies run a structured inventory for the first time, the total number of AI-related tools, embedded features, automations, and AI-enabled platforms operating across the business is typically two to three times higher than leadership's initial estimate (Alzahrani, 2025). The reason is not negligence. The reason is that AI is no longer confined to standalone "AI products." It is embedded throughout modern business software, often running quietly in the background without announcing itself.

Most companies already use platforms that incorporate AI in ways leadership has never invented as AI:

- CRM systems that score lead and forecast pipeline using machine learning.
- Email platforms that suggest replies, categorize messages, and route workflows automatically.
- Project management tools that predict completion dates and surface bottleneck patterns.
- Customer support systems with AI-driven routing, automated suggestions, and response generation.
- Productivity suites that have added "smart" features through routine

updates since 2023.

None of those entered the company as an AI implementation project. They arrived as features. That distinction changes how inventory and governance must work. If oversight is limited to tools explicitly purchased as "AI products," most of the actual AI surface area in the business will never get reviewed. Effective inventory means evaluating every software platform for AI-enabled functionality, automation, machine learning, or predictive components that influence decisions, customer interactions, internal workflows, or data handling.

Usage adds another layer of opacity. The subscription bill says twelve users. The reality might be that three of them use the platform daily, two used it twice and abandoned it, four have access but never activated, and three are department heads who pay for it as a courtesy. Financially they all look identical. Operationally, they are completely different, different values, different risks, different dependency. A subscription list cannot reveal that. An inventory must.

FIGURE 4.1 THE AI TOOL VISIBILITY PROBLEM

Most leaders only see a fraction of the AI tools actually operating in their business.

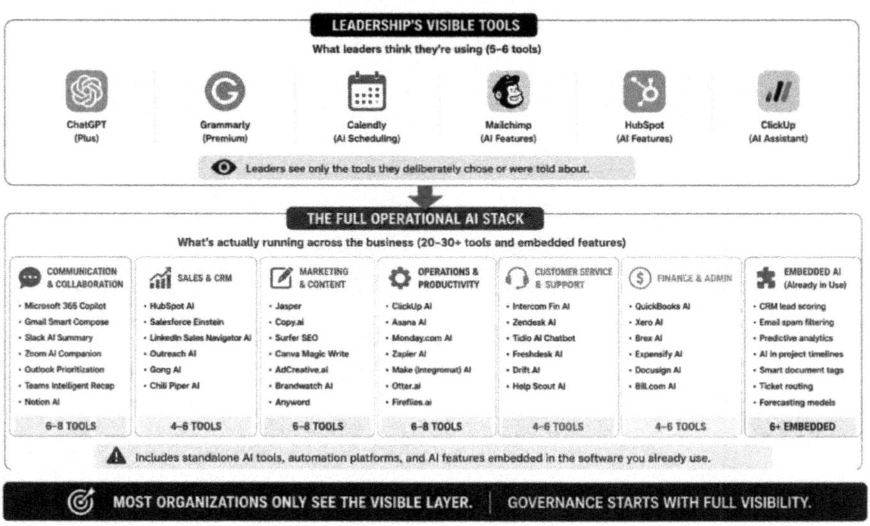

The accumulation is also gradual rather than strategic. AI rarely enters a company through one large implementation decision. It accumulates, one new feature, one employee experiment, one department pilot at a time — until leadership cannot answer basic questions: what systems are active, what data they process, who uses them, what outcomes they influence, what risks they introduce. Each individual decision was too small to formalize. The cumulative result is now too large to leave informal.

FIGURE 4.2 **HOW AI ACCUMULATES ACROSS THE BUSINESS**

AI enters your business from multiple directions over time—often in small, uncoordinated decisions.

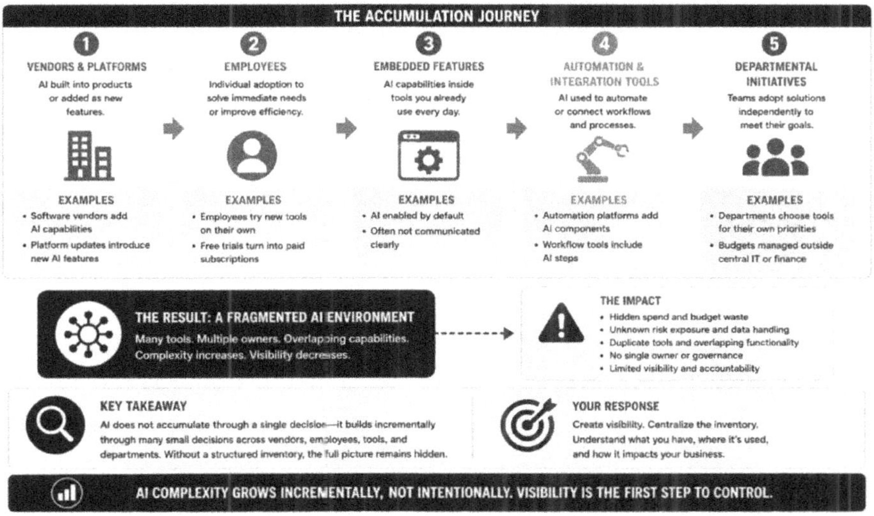

This chapter is about producing the artifact that closes that gap: a complete, current, operational inventory of every meaningful AI-related platform, feature, automation, and workflow operating across the business. The inventory becomes the visibility layer the rest of The AI Operating System™ depends on. Cost management, performance evaluation, risk assessment, governance — none of them work reliably without it.

The Complete AI Tool Inventory Framework

The framework is intentionally simple. Six standardized fields per tool. One row per tool. One centralized document. The simplicity is deliberate, because the inventory has to be maintainable for years, not just buildable once.

The inventory captures six core fields for every tool: tool name, business function, primary owner, monthly cost, contract terms, and current performance status.

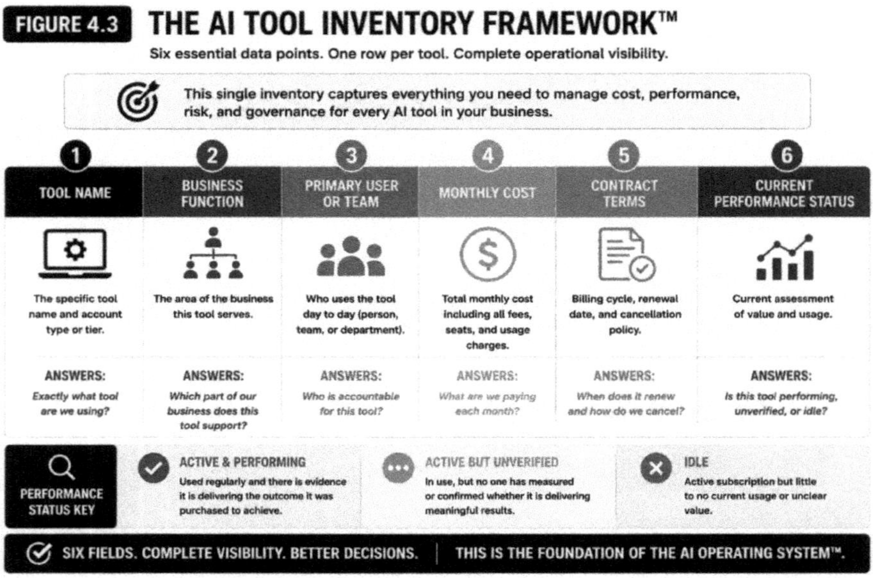

Tool name. Specificity matters more than most companies expect. "ChatGPT" is not specific enough, ChatGPT Plus, ChatGPT Team, and ChatGPT Enterprise carry different prices, administrative controls, security guarantees, and data-handling policies. The same applies to HubSpot, Salesforce, Microsoft 365, and every other platform with multiple tiers. Capture the exact product and tier.

Business function. Where the tool fits operationally. Use categories that match the company's actual structure, marketing, sales, customer service, operations, finance, administration, project management, HR. Tools supporting multiple functions get a primary classification and a note on secondary usage.

Primary user or team. Specific people, not vague departments. "Marketing" is not an owner. "Sarah Chen, content lead" is. Without a named owner, tools tend to remain active long after they have stopped delivering value because no one feels responsible for evaluating them.

Monthly cost. Fully loaded. Base subscription, usage charges, seat licenses, premium features, and any variable billing components. If costs fluctuate month to month, use the three-month average. Annual subscriptions get converted to a monthly figure so everything can be compared on the same scale. This field produces one of the most important outputs of the whole inventory: total AI spend per month and per year, on one page (Poon et al., 2025).

Contract terms. One of the largest gaps is the inventory usually surfaces. Document term length, renewal date, cancellation notice required, and whether pricing scales with usage. Auto-renewals on tools that have stopped delivering value are a predictable, expensive finding. So is the discovery that a tool the business is operationally dependent on is on a month-to-month vendor contract with thirty days' notice. Either condition is fine, provided leadership knows about it.

Current performance status. Three labels:

Active and performing — used regularly, producing measurable operational benefit.

Active but Unverified — currently in use, no formal performance evaluation has occurred (Soomro et al., 2025).

Idle — active subscription, minimal or no operational usage.

Most first-time inventories surface a meaningful number of idle and unverified tools. Those are the easiest cost reductions the audit will produce.

Six fields. One row per tool. The framework is lightweight on purpose. Elaborate scoring systems and technical assessment models do not survive long in operating businesses. A spreadsheet that gets updated does.

FIGURE 4.5 THE SIX FIELDS IN ACTION

How the AI Tool Inventory drives decisions, accountability, and business impact across the organization.

How to build the inventory

Schedule one focused on a three-hour working session. Before it starts, pull credit card statements, software billing records, accounting exports, and any centralized procurement records covering the last three months. Open a shared spreadsheet using the six fields above. The objective of the session is information capture — not evaluation, not optimization, not decision-making.

Work in three passes:

Pass 1 — Known tools. Document every AI-related platform leadership already knows about. Do not pause to research missing details. Capture what is known. Mark gaps.

Pass 2 — Financial records. Review credit cards and software billing line by line. Every unfamiliar vendor or recurring software charge gets added to the inventory. Many tools that arrived through employee adoption surface here for the first time (Sadiq et al., 2021).

Pass 3 — Existing platforms. Walk through core business platforms, CRM, project management, email, accounting, support, collaboration — and check each for embedded AI features. Most companies underestimate how much AI is already inside platforms they were using before AI was a topic.

After the session, the gaps systematically close over the next five business days. Vendor portals supply contract terms. Billing records supply cost details. Direct follow-up with employees supplies ownership and usage detail. Treat unresolved fields as open tasks until completed. A complete inventory with minimal uncertainty is substantially more valuable than a partial inventory full of assumptions.

Where inventory lives matter. A shared Google Sheet, a controlled SharePoint document, or a managed project-management database all work — provided ownership is defined and edits are tracked. An inventory edited inconsistently by everyone and maintained by no one stops being an inventory.

Categorizing Tools by Business Function and Dependency Level

A flat inventory creates visibility. It does not yet support decision-making. A spreadsheet with sixty tools, sixty owners, and sixty monthly costs is more information than the company had before, but it does not tell leadership which tools are critical, which are duplicative, and which deserve governance attention first. Categorization closes that gap.

Two layers transform the inventory into a management map: function grouping and dependency tiering.

Function grouping

Group every tool by the business function it supports. The function field is already in inventory; now review the groupings collectively rather than tool by tool. Two patterns almost always emerge:

Concentration. Some functions carry heavy AI investment while others are barely supported. Is the distribution aligned with where the business creates value? Marketing often shows large concentration because AI writing tools are widely available; operations and finance often show light concentration because the relevant tools require more integration work. Whether either condition is the right one depends on the company. The point is that the picture is now visible.

Overlap. Multiple tools inside the same function do the same thing. Two AI writing platforms in marketing. Three scheduling assistants across the company. Two meeting transcription services run on different teams. Overlap is the most predictable finding in this exercise and the easiest cost reduction the company will offer.

Dependency tiering

Dependency measures how much operational disruption would happen if the tool disappeared tomorrow. Three tiers:

FIGURE 4.6 DEPENDENCY TIER FRAMEWORK

Classify every AI tool by operational dependency to prioritize governance, risk management, and investment decisions.

Tier 1 — Critical. Embedded inside essential workflows. If the platform went away, core processes would fail or stall. Client deliverables stop. Operations break. Employees lack realistic alternatives. Tier 1 tools require the highest governance attention and the strongest vendor-risk evaluation (Westover, 2025; Hao et al., 2025). They also require contingency planning — what is the backup if the vendor changes pricing, terms, or availability?

Tier 2 — Operational. Meaningful productivity contribution, not essential to continuity. Losing them would cause inconvenience and friction, but the business would keep operating. Tier 2 tools need regular review and cost justification; they do not need the same governance intensity as Tier 1.

Tier 3 — Supplemental. Occasional use, narrow scope, easy to replace. Often the lowest governance priority, and frequently the easiest cost cuts.

Assigning tires is simpler than it sounds. For each tool, one question: if this disappeared tomorrow, what actually breaks? Major operational disruption is Tier 1. Manageable inconvenience is Tier 2. Minimal impact is Tier 3.

Add one more field while categorizing: a *redundancy flag*. Mark any tool that overlaps significantly with another inside the same function. The flag does not force a consolidation decision now. It just makes the overlap visible for the cost-review phase that follows.

Once every tool carries a function category, a dependency tier, and (where applicable) a redundancy flag, the inventory has become an operational map. Leadership now has a structured view of where AI is concentrated, where dependency exposure is highest, where consolidation is available, and where governance should focus first. The view is the asset.

FIGURE 4.7 THE AI GOVERNANCE DECISION FRAMEWORK™

Use the inventory data to make consistent, informed, and accountable decisions for every AI tool.

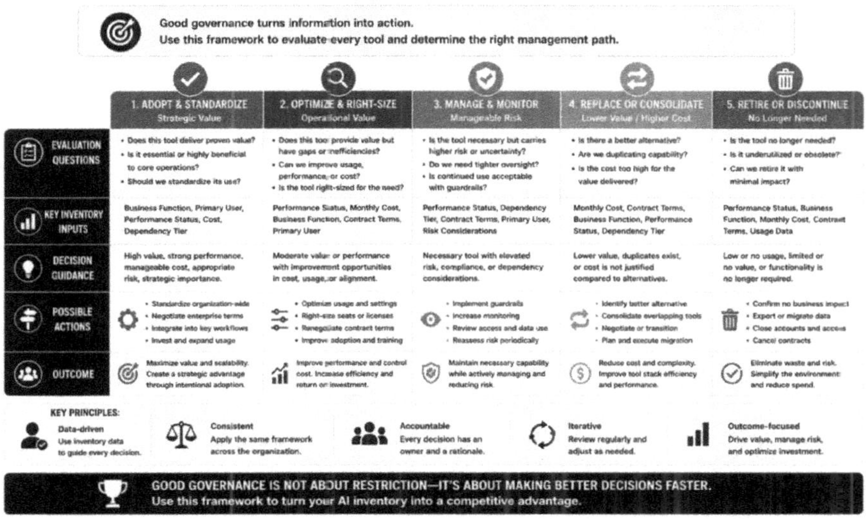

Three quick checks before moving on

Tier 3 spends. What share of total monthly AI spend is going to Tier 3 tools? A high share usually means there are immediate consolidation wins available with no operational disruption.

Tier 1 verification. Does every Tier 1 platform have an active performing status, that is, has its operational value been verified? If a tool the business cannot function without is in 'Active but Unverified' status, that is the most urgent performance review on the list.

Redundancy clusters. Are the flagged overlaps clustered in a few functions, or are they spread across many? Concentrated overlaps usually represent a single bad procurement pattern that is worth understanding before consolidating the tools.

Putting It into Practice

By this point the inventory has moved from being a project to being the operating foundation for every AI management decision that follows. The work in this section is the operating version of the framework, what to do in the next two weeks, in the order that produces the most clarity per hour of effort.

Within the next week — build the initial inventory. Schedule a three-hour working session. Gather credit card statements, software billing records, accounting exports, and any centralized procurement records covering the last three months. Using the six-field framework, capture every known AI-related platform, embedded feature, automation, and workflow operating inside the business. Do not pause for evaluation or consolidation decisions. By the end of the session, every identifiable tool is documented, and every remaining gap is marked.

Within five business days — close the gaps. Resolve missing fields systematically. Contract terms come from vendor portals or original agreements. Monthly cost comes from billing records. Owner and usage come from direct conversation. Treat unresolved fields as open tasks. A complete inventory with minimal uncertainty is substantially more valuable than a partial one full of assumptions.

Within ten business days — categorize. In one focused session, assign function and dependency tier to every tool, and flag any redundancy you find. This step is faster than people expect once the inventory exists, usually ninety minutes to two hours, and the operational clarity it produces is the highest-leverage output of the whole exercise.

Immediately after we produced three operational outputs.

Total monthly and annual AI spend. One number, on one page. Visible in every future budgeting and vendor review.

Tier 3 idle/marginal list. Cancellation, consolidation, or removal candidates. Acting on these is usually the first cost win of the audit.

Tier 1 unverified list. Tools the business depends on whose value has not been formally measured. These become the highest-priority performance reviews when Chapter 6 work begins.

When those four stages are done, the company has something most companies its size do not have: a documented, current, and actively maintained picture of every AI system operating across the business, with categorized priorities and immediately actionable findings. Decisions about AI stop happening reactively. They start happening against a baseline.

FIGURE 4.8 REVIEWING THE INVENTORY: LEADERSHIP PERSPECTIVES

Evaluate your AI inventory through six critical lenses to ensure balanced governance, value delivery, and risk control.

That shift, from reactive accumulation to deliberate management, is the central purpose of this chapter. The rest of the framework is built on top of it.

Chapter 5: The Real Cost of AI

Mapping What You're Actually Spending

CHAPTER OUTCOMES

At the end of this chapter, you will be able to:

- **Explain why AI spending is almost always higher than expected** – Understand how AI costs accumulate through subscriptions, usage, add-ons, and hidden labor.
- **Build a complete AI Cost Map** – Capture base subscriptions, variable usage, integrations and add-ons, and internal labor for every tool.
- **Calculate true cost of ownership** – Combine all cost components to determine the fully loaded monthly and annual cost for each tool.
- **Identify cost drivers and spending patterns** – Spot the tools, features, and usage behaviors that drive the highest costs.
- **Differentiate value from waste** – Identify tools that deliver measurable ROI and those draining budget without meaningful impact.
- **Establish a financial baseline for AI** – Create a documented total AI spend benchmark across the business for ongoing management.
- **Understand contract and renewal impact** – Track renewal dates, auto-renewals, and pricing escalations to avoid costly surprises.
- **Assign cost ownership and accountability** – Ensure every AI tool has a named owner responsible for cost management and value.
- **Reduce unnecessary spend** – Eliminate idle tools, consolidate redundancy, and right-size usage to lower total AI spend.
- **Use cost insight to fund what matters** – Reinvest savings into high-impact AI capabilities that drive measurable business results.

You can't manage what you don't measure. A complete cost map turns fragmented spend into strategic investment.
Know the cost. Control the spend. Maximize the value.

Why AI Costs Are Almost Always Higher Than You Think

AI spending rarely enters a business through one large, visible investment. It accumulates. One employee subscribes to a writing assistant. A department upgrades a project management platform to unlock AI features. Marketing adds a specialized automation tool. Operations adopt a workflow assistant whose pricing scales with usage rather than seats. Each decision looks reasonable in isolation. None of them gets reviewed against the others. None of them lands in a single budget conversation.

Then leadership tries to answer a basic question, what does AI cost the business each month, and discovers that the answer is harder to produce than it should be.

Most companies underestimate their AI spend during the first review. It is rarely that any single tool is expensive. The issue is that leadership has no consolidated view of how many AI-related expenses now exist simultaneously, and the actual total — once everything is mapped — is usually several times higher than the pre-audit estimate (Poon et al., 2025). The gap between perceived AI spend and actual AI spend is one of the most consistent findings in operational reviews.

FIGURE 5.1 How AI Costs Accumulate Quietly

How small operational decisions gradually create large unmanaged AI spending across the organization.

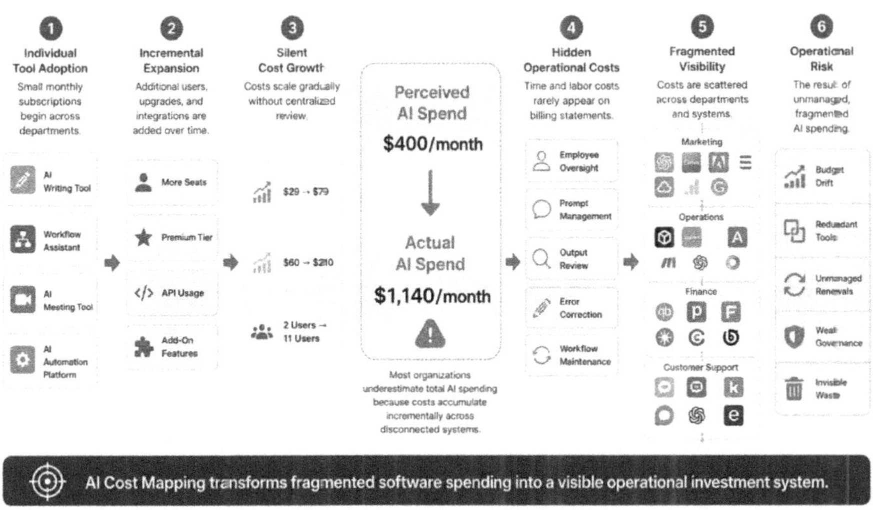

Modern AI pricing is part of the reason. Traditional software ran on predictable subscriptions — fixed fee, fixed user count, fixed month. AI platforms increasingly do not. Most combine a baseline subscription with one or more variable components: usage-based charges, premium feature tiers, overage fees, API consumption, storage costs, seat expansion, workflow execution fees, integration add-ons (Kar & Kushwaha, 2021). Costs scale dynamically with adoption. A $49-per-month platform that solved a single problem for one employee at adoption can become a $1,200-per-month operational expense after multiple teams build it into their workflows. None of the increases trigger a procurement review, because none of the increases looked large on their own.

The complexity extends beyond direct vendor billing. Some of the most significant AI-related costs never show up in accounting software at all. Operating an AI tool requires labor — time spent learning the platform, building prompts, reviewing outputs, correcting errors, maintaining configurations, troubleshooting automations, and integrating results into existing workflows (Hansen et al., 2024). The labor cost is distributed across employee time rather than centralized in a budget line, which is exactly why it is easy to miss. In practice, some businesses discover their labor oversight costs exceed the direct subscription costs entirely.

This chapter is about closing that visibility gap. The objective is not just to calculate total AI spend for accounting purposes. It is to build the cost framework that allows leadership to know where AI money is going, which tools justify their cost, and where spending is quietly drifting upward without anyone deciding it should. Once that picture exists, the conversation changes — AI becomes a managed investment portfolio rather than a fragmented collection of software charges (Westover, 2025).

The AI Tool Inventory built in Chapter 4 is the foundation. Every tool on that inventory carries some cost — direct, indirect, fixed, variable, or labor. The job of this chapter is to surface those costs and put them in one place.

FIGURE 5.2 **The AI Cost Map Framework™**

A complete view of the true monthly cost and expected value of every AI tool in your stack.

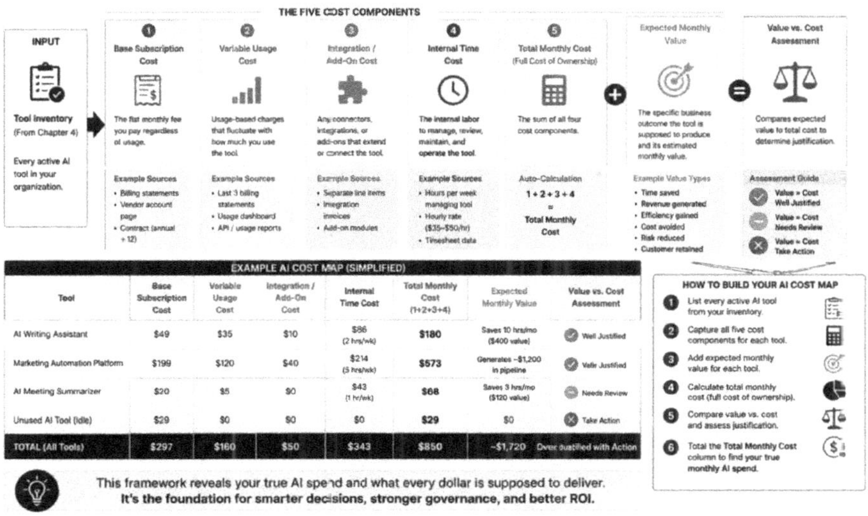

EXAMPLE AI COST MAP (SIMPLIFIED)

Tool	Base Subscription Cost	Variable Usage Cost	Integration / Add-On Cost	Internal Time Cost	Total Monthly Cost (1+2+3+4)	Expected Monthly Value	Value vs. Cost Assessment
AI Writing Assistant	$49	$35	$10	$86 (2 hrs/wk)	**$180**	Saves 10 hrs/mo ($400 value)	Well Justified
Marketing Automation Platform	$199	$120	$40	$214 (5 hrs/wk)	**$573**	Generates ~$1,200 in pipeline	Well Justified
AI Meeting Summarizer	$20	$5	$0	$43 (1 hr/wk)	**$68**	Saves 3 hrs/mo ($120 value)	Needs Review
Unused AI Tool (Idle)	$29	$0	$0	$0	**$29**	$0	Take Action
TOTAL (All Tools)	$297	$160	$50	$343	$850	~$1,720	Over-Justified with Action

Building Your AI Cost Map

The AI Cost Map is the financial twin of the inventory. The inventory says what exists. The Cost Map says what each item actually costs to keep running, fully loaded.

Building it well usually takes one focused three-hour working session, plus a small amount of vendor and billing follow-up afterward. The work happens against the existing inventory: add a cost-analysis section to every row and evaluate each tool against four cost categories.

Base subscription. The fixed monthly fee for access. Verify the exact billing structure rather than relying on memory, annual contracts dressed up as monthly figures, promotional pricing that has expired, and tier upgrades made mid-year are all common. Convert annual agreements to a monthly equivalent so every tool compares on the same scale.

Variable usage. The most difficult category to evaluate is because the structure varies by vendor. API requests, documents processed, workflow executions, storage consumption, generated outputs, query frequency, any of these may produce charges above the baseline. Pull at least three billing cycles for each tool and average them. Most vendors expose detailed usage dashboards that show exactly what generated the variable charges, which is worth checking before assuming the platform has been operating at "normal" levels.

Integration and add-on. Frequently overlooked because the charges often arrive on a separate invoice. Premium integrations, automation connectors, API bridge services, workflow extensions, enhanced security modules, collaboration upgrades, reporting features. Individually they look minor. Cumulatively they often add 20–40% to the headline subscription cost.

Internal labor. The most underestimated cost in the inventory. AI tools still need people, to operate them, review outputs, correct mistakes, maintain prompts, supervise automations. Estimate weekly hours per tool across direct users, reviewers, and administrators, convert to a monthly total, and multiply by a conservative blended hourly rate for the staff involved. The calculation is directional, not precise, but it consistently reveals that labor cost represents a substantial portion of total cost of ownership, often more than the subscription itself.

Once the four categories are populated for every tool, totaling the monthly cost of ownership becomes simple. Roll the per-tool totals up to a master summary. For most companies completing this for the first time, the final number lands meaningfully higher than leadership expected — usually because the variable, integration, and labor components were invisible before they were measured.

Adding the value side

Cost alone is not management. Cost paired with expected value is.

Add one more column to the Cost Map: *expected monthly value*. For every tool, identify the primary business outcome it is supposed to produce, and estimate the monthly value of that outcome. Some tools produce labor savings. Others speed up proposals, improve customer retention, increase reporting throughput, accelerate workflow completion. The point is not perfect financial forecasting.

The point is a reasonable estimate of whether each tool creates more business value than it consumes (Badghish & Soomro, 2024).

With cost and value side by side, the picture sharpens fast. Tools delivering strong returns become candidates for protection, expansion, or improved measurement. Tools delivering unclear value become candidates for performance review. Tools delivering nothing measurable become candidates for retirement. The map turns subscription pricing into something it has not been until now: a decision-grade financial framework.

Identifying Waste, Redundancy, and Silent Subscription Creep

With the Cost Map in place, the next step is using it as a management instrument rather than a financial record. Most avoidable AI spending falls into three patterns: waste, redundancy, and silent subscription creep. Each one is predictable. Each one is now visible.

FIGURE 5.3 **Waste, Redundancy & Subscription Creep**

The three operational spending patterns that quietly inflate AI costs across most organizations.

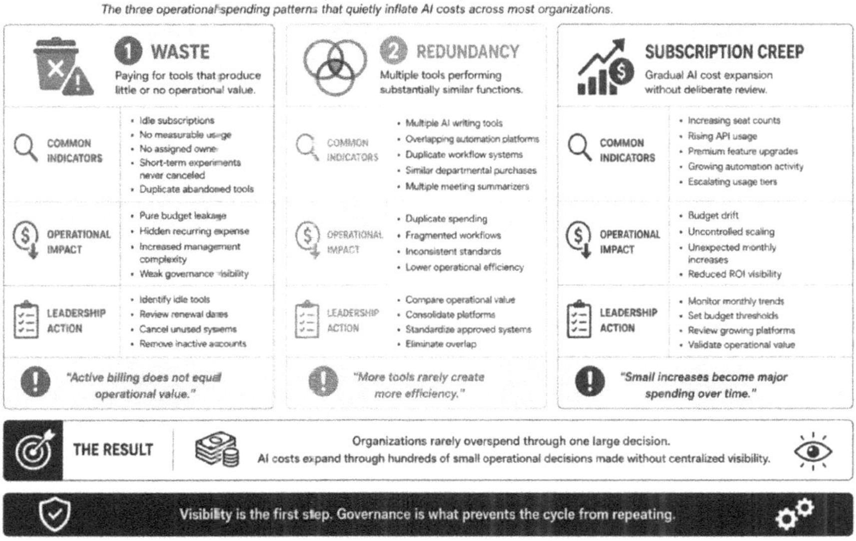

Waste

Waste is the easiest pattern to find — tools that continue to generate cost without producing operational value. Start with every platform classified as *Idle* in the Chapter 4 inventory. These tools have active subscriptions, ongoing billing, and minimal usage. They typically survived because nobody formally reviewed them after the initial experiment — an employee tested the platform, moved to a different tool, and never canceled the original. Build a cancellation review list. Note total monthly cost of ownership per tool. For most first-time audits, the cumulative annual cost of idle systems alone is enough to justify the whole exercise.

Redundancy

Redundancy is the next easiest pattern, and it tends to be the most expensive once aggregated. Multiple tools doing roughly the same job for the same team or workflow. Two AI writing platforms in marketing. Three scheduling assistants across departments. Two meeting transcription services running on different parts of the company. The redundancy almost always developed the same way: a tool was adopted to fill a gap, then a second tool was adopted later because someone preferred its interface or workflow, and the first tool was never retired.

To surface redundancy, go back to the function groupings from Chapter 4 and review each group as a set rather than tool by tool. Common redundancy clusters: AI writing assistants, content generation platforms, workflow automation systems, meeting transcription tools, scheduling assistants, reporting applications, customer communication platforms.

Do not rush to cancellation decisions at this stage. Flag the overlap in the Cost Map. Note which tool appears operationally dominant based on usage and integration depth. Consolidation decisions happen after performance review, not before — but the flag is what makes the eventual decision visible.

Silent subscription creep

The hardest pattern to recognize because the growth happens incrementally rather than as a discrete event. AI platforms scale their pricing as adoption deepens — additional users, expanded usage thresholds, premium feature unlocks, API volume increases. Each increase looks small in isolation. None of them lands as a single conspicuous price hike. Over time, the platform that entered the business at $49 a month is now billing $1,200 — and nobody made the decision to authorize the climb.

To surface creep, review at least three months of variable usage and subscription data for every tool. Tag each platform as *stable*, *growing*, or *declining*. Every tool tagged growing earns a closer look. The question is whether the cost growth reflects legitimate value expansion (more users, more output, more revenue activity supported) or whether the pricing simply scaled without corresponding business benefit. Either answer is fine, provided leadership has made the call deliberately rather than passively.

Once waste, redundancy, and creep are all visible, the conversation shifts. The pattern most companies experience for the first time is that AI cost growth has been *passive* rather than intentional — accumulating through dozens of individual reasonable decisions that were never evaluated collectively. That collective evaluation is what the Cost Map produces.

Three action categories

Group the findings into three action lists that become the basis for the next phase of work:

Cancellation candidates. Idle systems. Action: remove with minimal operational analysis.

Consolidation review candidates. Redundancy clusters. Action: performance comparison, then consolidate to the strongest tool.

Performance validation candidates. Growing systems. Action: verify the cost growth is producing matching business value before approving continued expansion.

For most companies, executing on these three categories alone produces material spend reduction without removing a single tool that is genuinely delivering value.

FIGURE 5.4 AI COST AUDIT WORKSHEET

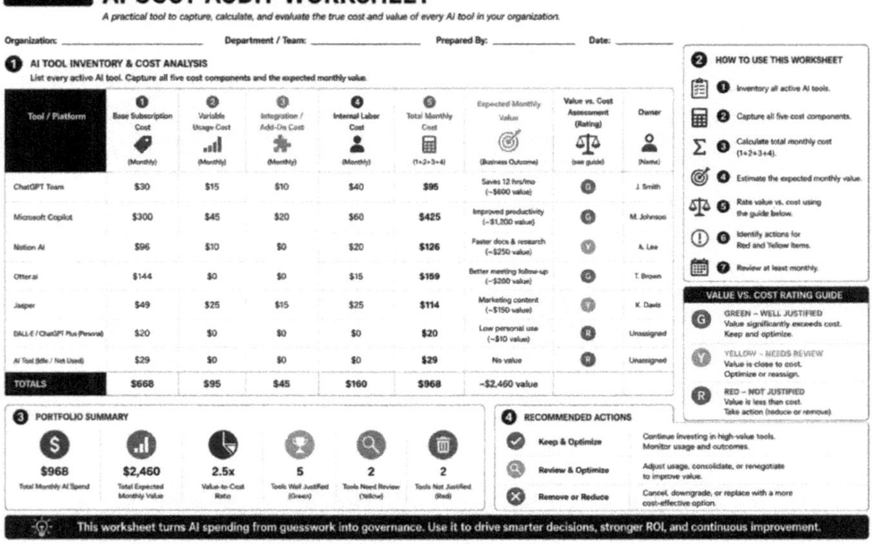

Setting a Baseline and a Budget Framework for AI Spending

Cost mapping and a first cleanup do not, by themselves, create lasting financial control. Companies that stop after the initial pass tend to drift back into the same fragmented spending pattern within nine to twelve months — new tools enter, usage scales, renewals fire, and the inventory quietly grows again. This section is about preventing that drift.

FIGURE 5.5 THE AI SPENDING GOVERNANCE FRAMEWORK™

The operational system that keeps AI spending visible, controlled, and aligned to business value.

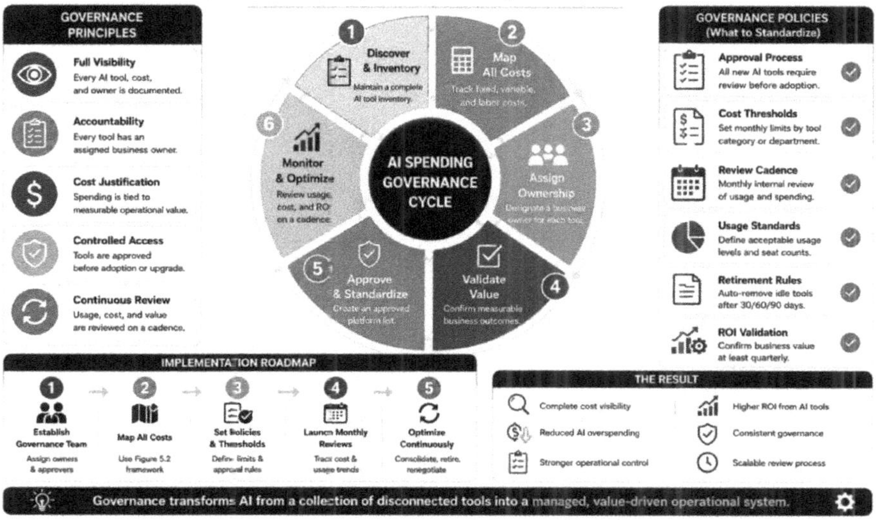

The objective is not a restrictive budget process. The objective is intentionality. AI spending should remain visible, deliberate, measurable, and tied to business priorities — without becoming an obstacle to legitimate experimentation.

Step 1 — Set the baseline.

The baseline is the company's intended operational AI spend after the cleanup. Take the total monthly cost from the completed Cost Map and subtract the monthly cost of every tool scheduled for cancellation, consolidation, or removal. The result is the post-optimization spending level. Document it. Add it to the monthly financial review as a managed line, not an incidental expense category.

That single act, moving AI from an aggregated category that no one tracks into a managed metric on a recurring agenda, is the single highest leverage change the framework introduces.

Step 2 — Build the budget framework around dependency tiers.

Each dependency tier from Chapter 4 (Critical / Operational / Supplemental) gets a different budget posture:

Tier 1 — Critical. Protected operational budget. Establish expected spending ranges for these systems based on current cost plus a 15–20% buffer for anticipated usage growth. Any Tier 1 cost increase that exceeds the buffer triggers an operational review — not to reject growth automatically, but to confirm the growth reflects real value expansion rather than vendor-driven price drift. If it does, update the baseline deliberately.

Tier 2 — Operational. Defined spending caps tied to current usage. Any Tier 2 system exceeding its approved threshold triggers a structured review. Tier 2 also receives recurring performance validation. A tool that stays active for two quarters without verified business value is consuming budget on inertia, and the framework should surface that pattern before it becomes structural.

Tier 3 — Supplemental. Strictest discipline. Every Tier 3 platform needs a named owner, a documented business purpose, and a verified outcome. If a Tier 3 tool cannot meet all three, it becomes an automatic review candidate at the next governance cycle.

Step 3 — Two organization-wide rules

Total spending ceiling. Set a maximum monthly AI spend relative to the baseline. A reasonable buffer allows experimentation; once total expenditure approaches the ceiling, additional platform expansion pauses until leadership reviews whether the increase is strategically justified.

Standardized approval gate. Every new AI tool now gets evaluated against three operational questions before purchase: is it useful, is it governable, and what is its impact on the overall spending structure? Adoption decisions stop happening in isolation; they happen against a budget.

Step 4 — Build review discipline into the existing rhythm

AI cost management does not work as an annual exercise. Add it to the monthly and quarterly cycles already in place.

Monthly check (15 minutes). Three questions:

Is total AI spending within the approved baseline range?

Have any systems exceeded their approved spending thresholds?

Are any major vendor renewals approaching that require performance validation before signing off?

Quarterly governance session (60 minutes). Deeper review:

Reassess the full Cost Map.

Update performance classifications.

Adjust dependency tiers where operational reality has shifted.

Identify accelerating cost trends.

Decide on renegotiation, consolidation, replacement, or removal for the next quarter.

The discipline is what prevents the framework from degrading. Without it, the baseline is accurate the day it gets set and obsolete six months later. With it, AI spending stays a managed category instead of becoming an uncontrolled one again.

The end state is straightforward to describe and uncommon to achieve. AI spending becomes a deliberate operational investment tied to measurable outcomes rather than a collection of disconnected vendor relationships drifting upward each quarter. Companies that maintain this discipline gain a structural advantage over peers who do not — the same spend, applied with intention, produces materially more business value.

Interlude: Converting Visibility into Action

A bridge between the diagnostic chapters (1–5) and the management chapters (6–12).

By this point in the book, the diagnostic work is done. The inventory exists. The cost map is built. Waste, redundancy, and subscription creep are visible. The business has — for the first time — a defensible picture of what AI is doing inside it.

Visibility is the foundation. It is not yet the result.

The next five chapters turn the diagnostic into a management system. Each one addresses a discipline the audit surfaced but did not yet solve:

Performance (Chapter 6) — turning the inventory into measurable business value, with scorecards, ROI evaluation, and review triggers.

Risk (Chapter 7) — converting the risk map into governance priorities and assigned accountability for consequential AI outputs.

Governance (Chapter 8) — writing the policies, approval processes, and data-handling standards that make the framework durable.

Alignment (Chapter 9) — making sure every active tool earns its place against the business's actual strategic priorities.

Integration (Chapter 10) — embedding AI into real workflows rather than running it parallel to them.

Before any of those chapters fully land, the work from Chapters 1–5 needs to be *executed*, not just understood. Visibility that sits in a spreadsheet does not change how the business operates. Visibility drives cancellations, consolidations, performance reviews, and a defended baseline does.

The ten-day execution rhythm:

Days 1–3. Complete the Cost Map across all four cost categories. Document expected monthly value per tool. Produce the consolidated AI spending baseline number.

Days 4–5. Surface the three spending patterns: idle systems (waste), overlapping systems (redundancy), and systems with growing cost trends (creep). Tag each.

Day 6. Execute the first round of decisions. Cancel idle systems before their next renewal. Schedule consolidation for redundancy clusters. Document justification or a corrective action, for every growing cost system.

Days 7–9. Set the post-cleanup baseline. Apply the tier-aligned budget framework. Establish the spending ceiling. Stand up the approval gate. Add the monthly check to the leadership cadence.

Day 10. Put the first quarterly AI cost governance review on the calendar ninety days out. The framework's durability depends on the recurring rhythm, not on the initial cleanup.

When those ten days are complete, the company has done something most companies its size has not: it has converted a one-time audit into a managed operational discipline. Chapters 6 through 12 are about extending that discipline across the rest of the AI function, performance, risk, governance, alignment, integration, decision-making, and the recurring operating rhythm that ties them all together.

Begin the ten-day rhythm now. Then turn the page.

At that point, AI-related expenses stop functioning as fragmented vendor charges hidden across departments, workflows, and billing systems. Artificial intelligence becomes a visible operational investment category with measurable costs, defined governance controls, structured review processes, and clear expectations regarding business value creation.

Chapter 6: AI Performance Governance™

Moving from Assumptions to Measurable Business Value

CHAPTER OUTCOMES

At the end of this chapter, you will be able to:

- Measure AI system performance consistently across four key dimensions.
- Calculate the true ROI and total cost of ownership for every AI tool.
- Establish performance benchmarks and triggers that drive action.
- Implement a recurring governance review rhythm to ensure ongoing value.
- Identify underperforming systems and make data-driven decisions to optimize your AI portfolio.
- Create a culture of continuous improvement and accountable AI investment.

Most owners have a general sense that their AI tools are helping. Work feels faster. Teams look more efficient. Tasks that took hours now take minutes. The perception is usually directionally right. Perception is not performance measurement.

Once meaningful spending, operational reliance, and decision-making are attached to AI systems, the burden shifts. Impressions are no longer enough to justify continued investment, and they will not support the kind of management decision the business eventually has to make about which tools to keep, expand, or retire.

The problem in most companies is not that AI ROI is hard to calculate. The problem is that almost no AI system gets evaluated through a structured performance framework (Sadiq et al., 2021). Tools are adopted quickly, embedded into workflows informally, and allowed to continue operating without consistent benchmarks or owners. Time savings are assumed rather than measured. Quality is judged on whether outputs feel "good enough." Subscription costs renew month after month without anyone asking whether the value is still there.

The challenge gets harder in small and mid-sized companies because almost none of them documented a baseline before AI adoption started. Nobody timed the task before it was automated. Nobody measured the error rate before AI-generated outputs entered the workflow. When leadership later wants to evaluate whether a tool is actually working, there is no "before" to compare against.

This chapter is about closing that gap.

Companies cannot govern performance they have never defined, and they cannot improve systems they never measure. The frameworks below establish a practical, repeatable method for evaluating every AI system on the same criteria — regardless of function, department, or vendor. The goal is not financial precision. The goal is consistent visibility into measurable business value (Soomro et al., 2025). Once that visibility exists, the budget conversation stops being about which tools feel useful and starts being about which ones can be defended.

The AI Performance Scorecard™

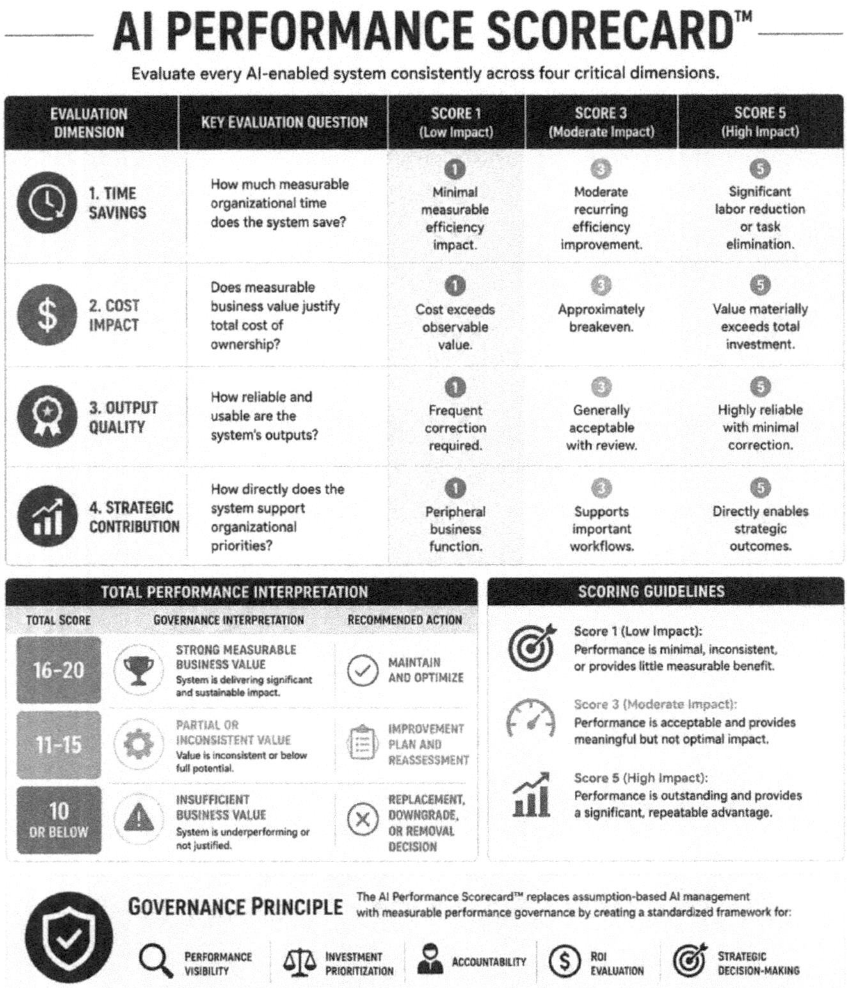

Figure 6.1 — AI Performance Scorecard™.

The AI Performance Scorecard™ evaluates every active AI system across the same four dimensions: *time savings*, *cost impact*, *output quality*, and *strategic contribution*. Each dimension is scored 1 to 5. Total ranges from 4 to 20.

Consistency is the entire point. When every tool is evaluated on the same dimensions with the same scoring scale, leadership can compare across the AI environment using a common framework rather than tool-by-tool gut judgment. Patterns become visible quickly: which systems generate real business impact, which improve capacity, which consume resources inefficiently, and which are operating on assumption rather than evidence.

Run the scorecard against every active system. Not just the expensive ones. Not just the obvious ones. The most common surprise in this exercise is that some of the least expensive tools produce the strongest measurable value — and some of the highest-cost tools produce the weakest.

Dimension 1 — Time Savings

Measurable reduction in labor time compared to the process the system replaced. Compare how long the task took before, how long it takes now, and whether human review or correction offsets part of the gain. If no baseline was documented before adoption, use directional estimates from the primary users.

Score	Performance Level
1	Less than 30 minutes saved weekly
2	Moderate but inconsistent reduction
3	Two to four hours saved weekly
4	Significant recurring workflow acceleration
5	More than six hours saved weekly, or substantial task elimination

Figure 6.2 — Time Savings scoring guidelines

Dimension 2 — Cost Impact

Whether the measurable value created by the system justifies its total cost of ownership from Chapter 5 (subscription + variable + integration + labor). The question is comparative: value produced vs. cost consumed.

Score	Performance Level
1	Cost materially exceeds measurable value
2	Weak return relative to total investment
3	Approximately breakeven
4	Strong positive measurable return
5	Value creation exceeds total cost by at least 3×

Figure 6.3 — Cost Impact scoring guidelines

Dimension 3 — Output Quality

How reliable, accurate, usable, and trustworthy the system's outputs are inside real workflows. Evaluate consistency, accuracy, correction frequency, review burden, and the confidence level the team has when relying on the output. A system producing large volumes of low-quality work that needs heavy human cleanup produces the appearance of efficiency while degrading effectiveness.

Quality is not static. Governance research describes the gradual decline of AI output reliability as *model drift* — changing data patterns, evolving workflows, or shifting usage conditions slowly erode performance after deployment. A system that scores 4 today can drift to 2 in eighteen months without anyone noticing. That is why output quality has to be reassessed on a recurring basis rather than locked in at adoption.

Score	Performance Level
1	Frequent errors or significant rework required
2	Inconsistent reliability
3	Generally acceptable with regular review
4	Consistently strong with limited correction

Figure 6.4 — Output Quality scoring guidelines

Dimension 4 — Strategic Contribution

How directly does the system supports a meaningful business priority. This is the dimension most often overlooked, and it is where the real distinction between "convenient" and "strategically valuable" gets drawn. A tool can produce solid efficiency without supporting anything that matters to the business — and a tool can produce modest efficiency while enabling a critical strategic outcome. The score should reflect alignment with revenue, scalability, retention, capacity, cost reduction, competitive positioning, or other defined organizational priorities.

Score	Performance Level
1	Peripheral or low-impact function
2	Limited connection to business priorities
3	Supports an important business function
4	Strong alignment with organizational objectives
5	Directly enables critical strategic outcomes

Figure 6.5 — Strategic Contribution scoring guidelines

Interpreting the total score

Total Score	Governance Interpretation
16-20	Strong measurable business value. Maintain and optimize.
11-15	Partial value. Improvement plan or targeted review required.
10 or below	Insufficient measurable value. Immediate decision required.

Figure 6.6 — Performance score interpretation

Systems scoring 10 or below should not stay active indefinitely without documented justification, an improvement plan, or a replacement decision. Performance governance requires the company to make a call when the evidence says one is needed.

Calculating True AI ROI Without a Finance Degree

ROI answers a simple question: *Is the company receiving more measurable value than it is investing?* Most AI environments never get a real answer. The calculation is skipped entirely, or it is done with assumptions narrow enough to miss the actual business impact in either direction.

The most common small-business shortcut is straightforward:

time saved × hourly rate, compared to subscription cost.

That is a reasonable starting point and an inadequate ending one. A governance-grade ROI calculation includes four inputs:

Net labor efficiency. Time saved minus correction time. A system that saves five hours but requires two hours of review produces three hours of net efficiency, not five (Hansen et al., 2024).

Output quality impact. Measurable improvements in client experience, proposal quality, reporting accuracy, response time, or retention. Use directional estimates when precise dollar values are unavailable.

Error cost exposure. The cost of AI errors reaching clients, decisions, financial reports, or regulated communications, correction labor, client remediation, reputational drag, and the occasional direct financial hit (Hao et al., 2025).

Opportunity value creation. Whether the time the system saves gets redeployed to higher-value work — revenue generation, client development, strategic planning. If reclaimed hours disappear into general busyness, the system produces only a fraction of its potential value.

The AI ROI Evaluation Framework™

FIGURE 6.7 — AI ROI EVALUATION FRAMEWORK™

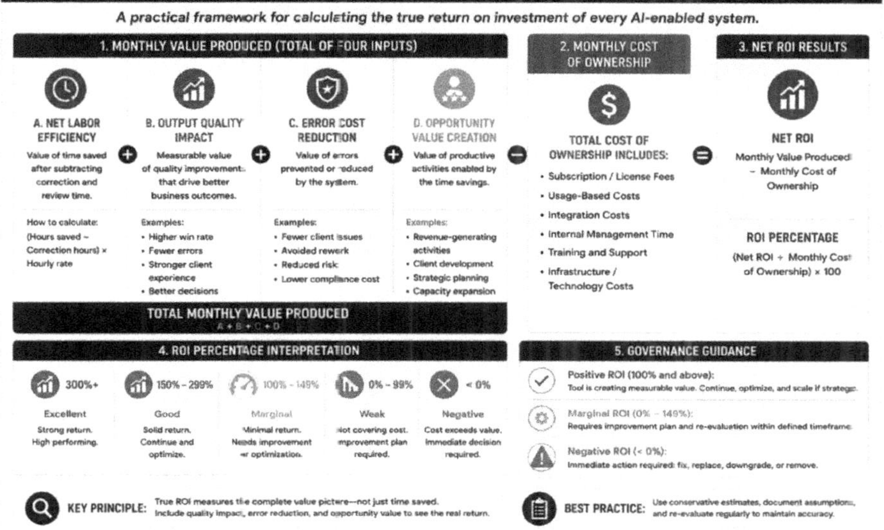

Monthly Value Produced = net labor efficiency + measurable quality improvements + measurable error reduction.

Monthly Cost of Ownership = subscription + variable usage + integration + internal labor (from Chapter 5).

Net Business Impact = Monthly Value Produced – Monthly Cost of Ownership.

ROI % = (Net Business Impact ÷ Monthly Cost of Ownership) × 100.

Examples: 150% ROI means $1.50 of value per $1.00 invested. 300% ROI means $3.00 of value per $1.00 invested. Negative ROI means the company is losing measurable value relative to investment.

Two principles to anchor the calculation.

Visibility matters more than precision. Directionally accurate ROI applied consistently across every system produces more useful governance than mathematically perfect ROI applied to one tool. Start with the five highest-cost systems, they carry the most financial exposure and the most upside and extend the framework across the rest of the inventory after the first pass.

Conservative assumptions create better governance. Avoid inflated efficiency estimates, exaggerated quality claims, and unrealistic productivity assumptions designed to justify continued usage. The point of the exercise is not to defend existing investments. The point is to surface which systems are creating real value and which are consuming resources without producing proportional outcomes.

Establishing Performance Benchmarks and Review Triggers

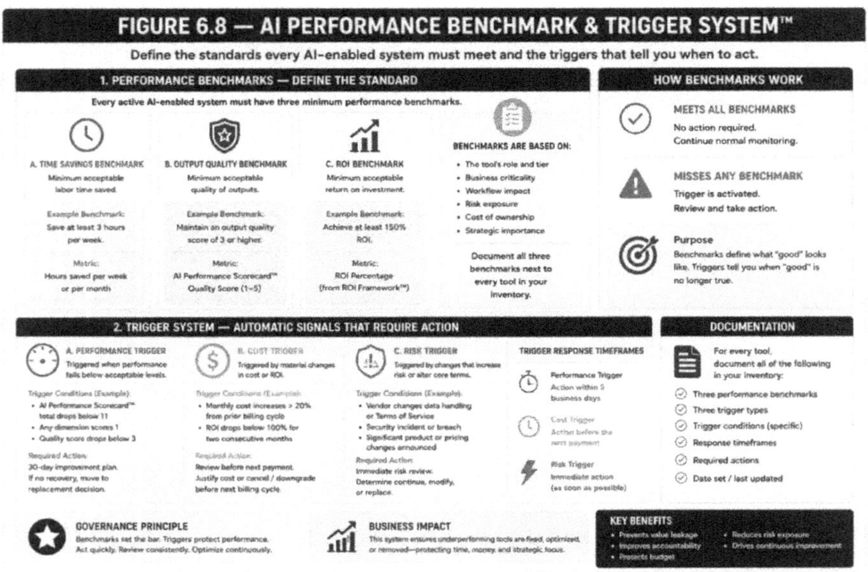

A single ROI calculation is a snapshot. Sustainable governance requires structure to detect when performance has changed enough to require leadership attention.

A *benchmark* is a clearly defined performance standard the system is expected to maintain — measurable, specific, tied to a business outcome. Examples: "saves at least three hours weekly," "maintains an output quality score of 4 or higher," "sustains positive ROI above 100%." When a system meets its benchmarks, no action is required. When it falls below them, a review fires.

Benchmarks do not need to be identical across systems. A client-facing tool may need stricter quality expectations than an internal draft assistant. A strategically important platform may justify lower short-term ROI if it materially improves capacity. The goal is accountability calibrated to business importance, not uniform standards.

A *review trigger* is a condition that requires immediate reassessment — rather than waiting for the next scheduled review. Three categories:

Performance trigger. Scorecard's total drops below the minimum threshold. Move the system into a structured improvement review. If measurable improvement does not occur within a defined remediation window, decide on replacement, downgrade, or removal.

Cost trigger. Material cost increase or sustained ROI decline across two review periods. Conduct an immediate financial reassessment before additional spending continues.

Risk trigger. Significant vendor policy changes, security incidents, pricing restructuring, or material changes to data-handling practices. These trigger reviews regardless of performance — a strong-performing system can still become unacceptable if its risk profile changes underneath it.

The review rhythm

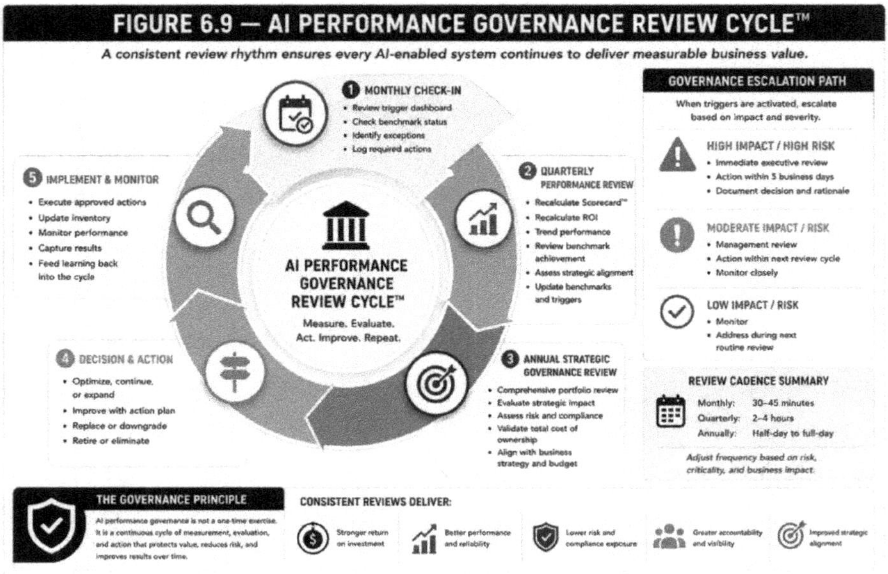

Trigger monitoring lives inside the monthly inventory review already established in Chapter 4. Fifteen minutes is enough.

Monthly. Check for triggered conditions. Note any system that has crossed a threshold.

Quarterly. Rerun the scorecard. Recalculate ROI for the high-cost systems. Reassess benchmark alignment. Update dependency tiers if usage has shifted.

Annually. Comprehensive governance refreshes strategic alignment, budget allocation, vendor dependency, and overall, AI performance maturity across the environment.

The structure is simple. The effectiveness comes from following through. The hardest part of performance governance is rarely defining a benchmark; it is making the call once the evidence shows the benchmark is no longer being met. Companies that consistently defer those calls end up running underperforming tools indefinitely. Companies that act on triggered evidence inside a defined window build governance discipline that sustains long-term business value (Westover, 2025).

Converting Performance Visibility into Governance Discipline

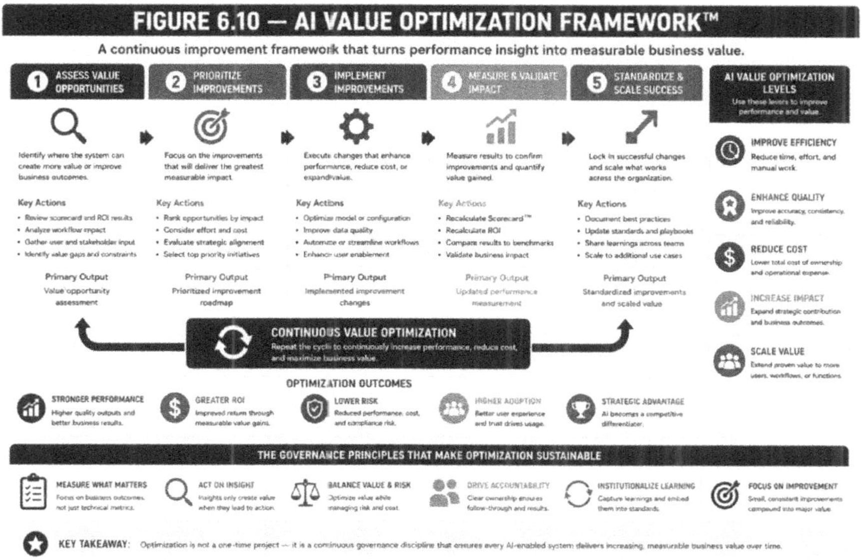

The frameworks in this chapter are only useful when they are run. The three-week implementation sequence:

Week 1 — Score every active system. Run the AI Performance Scorecard™ against every AI tool in the inventory. All four dimensions. Document scores directly inside the inventory document so each system has a baseline performance profile. Do not limit evaluation to expensive systems — some of the cheapest tools turn out to be the most strategically valuable, and some of the most expensive turn out to be the weakest.

Week 2 — ROI the top five. Calculate full-framework ROI for the five highest-cost AI systems using all four inputs (labor efficiency, quality impact, error cost, opportunity value). Document results in inventory. Any high-cost system with negative ROI gets a leadership review before the weekends are the most expensive places where assumption-based AI management is costing real money.

Week 3 — Set benchmarks and triggers. For every active system, document minimum acceptable performance thresholds: efficiency, output quality, and ROI. Document the three review triggers (performance / cost / risk). Add trigger monitoring to the monthly inventory review. Put the first quarterly performance governance review on the calendar ninety days out.

When the three weeks are done, AI performance evaluation stops being an annual hope and starts being a recurring management function. Leadership has documented performance baselines, measurable evaluation standards, structured review triggers, and a decision-making framework calibrated to the business's actual priorities. The system is not complicated. Its effectiveness comes from running it consistently, and from acting on what it reveals.

Chapter 7: AI Risk Management

Protecting Your Business Without Slowing It Down

CHAPTER OUTCOMES

At the end of this chapter, you will be able to:

- Identify and classify AI operational risk across data, decision, vendor dependency, and compliance exposure.
- Run a structured AI Operational Risk Assessment™ using the ten-question governance framework.
- Implement proportionate governance controls based on Low, Medium, and High-risk classifications.
- Build vendor dependency contingency plans for operationally critical AI systems.
- Establish AI Decision Accountability Framework™ controls for consequential AI outputs.
- Create a recurring governance reassessment process that keeps AI exposure visible and manageable over time.

Every company running AI is already managing risk — whether anyone has named it that way or not. AI systems shape customer communications, financial reporting, internal decisions, hiring screens, marketing operations, and data handling across nearly every function. As adoption expands, so does the exposure.

That exposure is not a reason to avoid AI. It is a reason to manage it deliberately.

The pattern is consistent. Employees adopt tools independently. Vendors quietly add AI features to platforms the business already pays for. Dependency deepens. Sensitive data starts moving through systems leadership has never reviewed. In most companies, AI is operationally embedded long before any governance structure exists around it (Sánchez et al., 2025). The risk has not been managed badly. It has not been managed at all.

The fix is structural, not heroic. Once exposure is documented concretely — what data, which vendors, which decisions, which regulatory commitments — most of it becomes manageable through ordinary review processes and proportionate controls. The framework below produces that documentation. By the end of the chapter, the business will have a structured method for evaluating AI risk, assigning ownership for consequential AI outputs, managing vendor dependency, and applying governance controls scaled to actual exposure.

None of this requires advanced technical expertise or enterprise-scale infrastructure. It requires operational discipline, clear ownership, and a structured approach. The companies that manage AI risk well are not the ones with the biggest tech budgets. They are the ones that established clarity before complexity got loose.

AI Operational Risk Categories™

AI exposure inside small and mid-sized businesses does not show up as a single threat. It develops across four overlapping categories: data risk, decision risk, vendor dependency risk, and compliance risk. Almost every operational risk scenario tied to AI traces back to one or more of these.

Figure 7.1 — AI Operational Risk Categories™

A structured framework for identifying and classifying AI-related organizational exposure across governance, accountability, vendor dependency, and compliance dimensions.

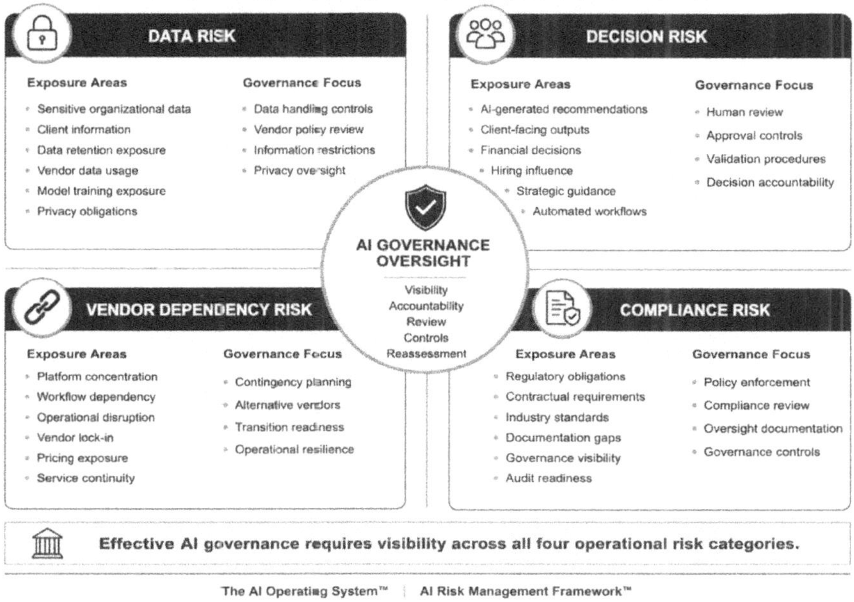

- **Data risk.** Information leaving the business through AI tools, including what is stored, retained, or used to train external models.
- **Decision risk.** AI outputs influencing consequential decisions, including financial, hiring, and customer-facing decisions, without defined review and ownership.
- **Vendor dependency risk.** Critical workflows reliant on a single AI vendor or platform without contingency planning.
- **Compliance risk.** AI usage conflicts with regulatory, contractual, or industry-specific obligations the business has accepted.

Data risk

When an employee passes a client contract into an AI summarizer, uploads a financial statement into an analysis tool, or runs an internal document through a chatbot, that data leaves the company's direct control. What happens next depends entirely on the vendor — retention policy, training rights, infrastructure controls, sub-processor disclosures, data sovereignty (where data is stored, across which jurisdictions, under whose laws). None of these vendor practices is necessarily malicious. All of them can conflict with client obligations, internal policies, contractual confidentiality, or regulatory requirements (Pumplun et al., 2019). Data risk scales directly with the sensitivity of the information moving through the system.

Decision risk

AI now participates in proposal drafting, pricing recommendations, hiring evaluations, customer communications, financial summaries, and operational analysis. The question is not whether AI systems make mistakes — every system does — but whether the business has review and ownership defined for the outputs that matter. Decision risk is high when AI outputs reach clients without review, when recommendations influence financial or employee decisions, or when leadership assumes AI-generated content is reliable by default. Decision risk is low when AI outputs are treated as *supporting inputs* that flow through a defined human review and approval step before anything consequential happens.

Vendor dependency risk

Vendor dependency is the least visible category and frequently the most operationally significant. It develops gradually — switching costs rise, employee habits solidify, integrations deepen, workflows assume continued availability. Eventually the vendor is operational infrastructure whether leadership intended that or not. Dependency exposure peaks when critical workflows rely on a single platform, data portability is limited, pricing changes, terms shift unexpectedly, or the vendor discontinues key functionality.

Compliance risk

Compliance risk varies by industry, geography, customer requirements, and the kind of data being processed. Companies in healthcare, financial services, legal, education, insurance, or government contracting carry heightened obligations around privacy, information handling, retention, automated decision-making, and operational transparency. Companies outside heavily regulated industries still carry contractual obligations governing customer data, employee data, and proprietary information. Compliance exposure increases sharply when leadership cannot answer the basic questions: what systems are running, what data they process, who has access, how outputs are reviewed.

These categories interact. A single customer-service AI platform may simultaneously carry data risk (handling customer information), decision risk (influencing complaint resolution), vendor dependency risk (only support workflow), and compliance risk (operating in a regulated industry). Separating the categories lets the company evaluate exposure precisely rather than treating AI risk as one undifferentiated concern.

Practical starting point: walk the AI inventory from Chapter 4. For each active system, mark which of the four categories apply. Do not rate severity yet. The first pass is just visibility — where exposure exists.

Running an AI Operational Risk Assessment™

The assessment does not require a legal team or specialized expertise. It requires the same ten governance questions applied consistently to every active AI system. The questions are scaled 1–5; the total produces a risk classification.

Figure 7.2 — The AI Operational Risk Assessment™

A 10-question methodology for evaluating AI-enabled tools based on operational impact, sensitivity exposure, dependency level, and compliance considerations.

#	RISK QUESTION	WHAT TO CONSIDER	SCORE (Circle One)
1	What types of data does this AI tool access or process?	Does it handle sensitive, confidential, client, financial, employee, or proprietary information?	0 1 2
2	Where is the data stored and how is it used?	Review vendor policies on data retention, storage location, third-party sharing, and model training usage.	0 1 2
3	Does this tool influence or generate outputs used for decisions?	Does it inform client deliverables, internal decisions, recommendations, or automated workflow outcomes?	0 1 2
4	What is the potential impact of an inaccurate or biased output?	Consider financial, legal, operational, reputational, or client impact if the output is wrong.	0 1 2
5	How critical is this tool to your operations?	Would workflows, client service, or internal processes be significantly disrupted if the tool became unavailable?	0 1 2
6	How dependent are you on this vendor?	Evaluate the availability of viable alternatives and the difficulty of switching vendors.	0 1 2
7	Does this tool create compliance or regulatory exposure?	Consider industry regulations, privacy laws, contractual obligations, and documentation requirements.	0 1 2
8	How transparent and explainable are the tool's outputs?	Can the outputs be verified, audited, and explained to stakeholders if needed?	0 1 2
9	What is the financial commitment and cost exposure?	Consider pricing model, usage variability, contract terms, and cost increases.	0 1 2
10	How well is the tool governed internally?	Are usage guidelines, access controls, human review, and documentation in place?	0 1 2

SCORING INSTRUCTIONS: 0 = Low Risk | 1 = Moderate Risk | 2 = High Risk

TOTAL SCORE ________ (Max Score: 20)

RISK LEVEL CLASSIFICATION

LOW RISK (0 – 6)	MEDIUM RISK (7 – 13)	HIGH RISK (14 – 20)
Minimal operational exposure. Standard oversight and documentation are sufficient. *Proceed with documented oversight.*	Moderate exposure requiring defined controls and management attention. *Implement mitigation within 60 days.*	Significant exposure requiring immediate governance, controls, and accountability. ***Implement mitigation within 30 days.***

PURPOSE: This assessment creates consistent visibility into AI-related operational risk so organizations can apply proportionate controls, strengthen governance, and reduce unmanaged exposure over time.

The AI Operating System™ | AI Risk Management Framework™

1 Does the system process sensitive customer, financial, or proprietary data?

2 Are AI outputs distributed externally without consistent human review?

3 Does the system influence financial, hiring, or operational decisions?

4 Is the business operationally dependent on a single vendor for this function?

5 Is there a viable replacement if the vendor disappears or changes terms?

6 Are vendor data-handling terms documented and understood?

7 Does the system operate in a regulated industry or under contractual confidentiality?

8 Could the system handle data that triggers HIPAA, GLBA, PCI, GDPR, or similar obligations?

9 Has the system been formally reviewed for accuracy, bias, or output reliability?

10 Is there a named human accountable for output quality and approval?

Total scores roll up to a classification:

Table 7.1 — Risk rating thresholds

Once classifications are assigned, governance attention concentrates where it matters. Low-risk systems get visibility and periodic review. Medium-risk systems get governance enhancement on a 60-day window. High-risk systems get immediate structured controls. The point is proportionality — applying the same level of oversight to every tool produces governance fatigue and exposes the business where attention is needed.

Vendor Dependency: Building a Practical Contingency Framework

Most companies discover vendor dependency exposure only after a problem already exists — a price hike that doubles the bill, a policy change that breaks the workflow, a service disruption that halts an entire team. The framework below makes the exposure visible before that point.

Figure 7.3 — AI Vendor Dependency Risk Model™

A framework for evaluating and managing dependence on AI vendors to protect operational continuity and reduce disruption risk.

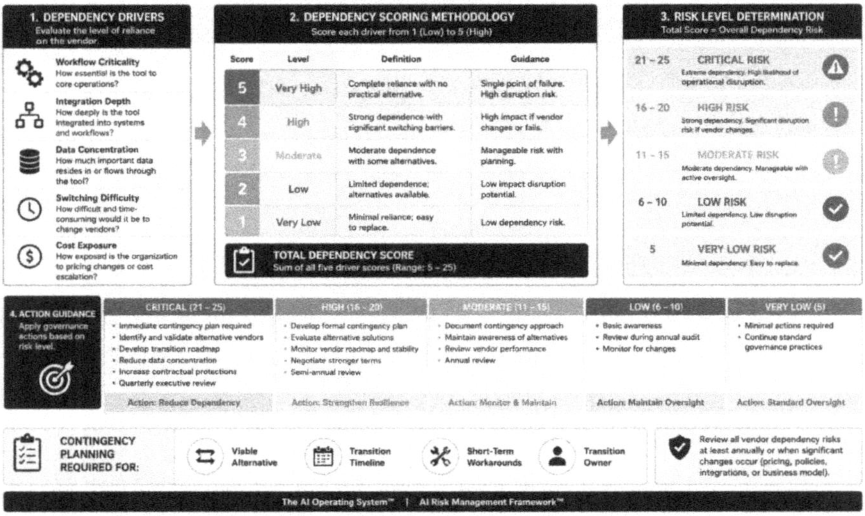

For every Tier 1 system carrying meaningful vendor dependency, document four elements in the inventory:

Viable alternative vendor. At least one realistic replacement platform capable of supporting the same function.

Estimated transition timeline. Implementation, workflow migration, employee onboarding, data transfer, process adjustment. Even a rough estimate is more useful than no estimate.

Operational impact assessment. Which workflows would be disrupted, delayed, or shifted to manual processing during a transition? Where do temporary workarounds exist?

Transition accountability owner. Named individual responsible for coordinating the transition if it becomes necessary.

The contingency documentation takes about thirty minutes per system. That investment moves the business from "there is a vendor we cannot live without" to "there is a vendor we operate with deliberately and could replace if we had to." The exposure does not disappear. Exposure becomes governable.

Vendor concentration also deserves a periodic look. As adoption expands, a single vendor often ends up supporting multiple business functions across departments. That concentration is fine — provided it is visible and deliberate. The quarterly governance review is the right place to ask whether any vendor now supports two or more critical functions, whether contingency plans are still current, and whether governance controls are still proportionate to actual exposure.

AI Decision Accountability: Establishing Human Oversight

One of the most persistent misconceptions about AI is the assumption that responsibility transfers to technology once it starts producing outputs. It does not (Yablonsky, 2021). When an AI-generated proposal goes to a client, the client holds the business accountable. When AI influences hiring or financial decisions, the consequences sit with the company. AI does not carry legal accountability, regulatory liability, or governance obligations. The business does.

Not every AI output requires the same level of oversight. Governance should be proportionate. Low-accountability uses include brainstorming, internal drafts, and preliminary research — outputs that depend heavily on human interpretation afterward. High accountability uses include outputs that directly influence:

Client-facing deliverables.

Financial decisions and reporting.

Employee-related actions (hiring, compensation, evaluation).

Operational recommendations and approvals.

Legal or contractual communications.

Regulatory reporting.

Strategic management decisions.

Any AI system whose outputs influence those categories should be classified a High-Accountability AI System and operate under the AI Decision Accountability Framework™, three controls applied consistently.

Figure 7.4 — AI Decision Accountability Framework™

A structured model for ensuring human accountability, oversight, and documented responsibility for AI-influenced decisions and outputs.

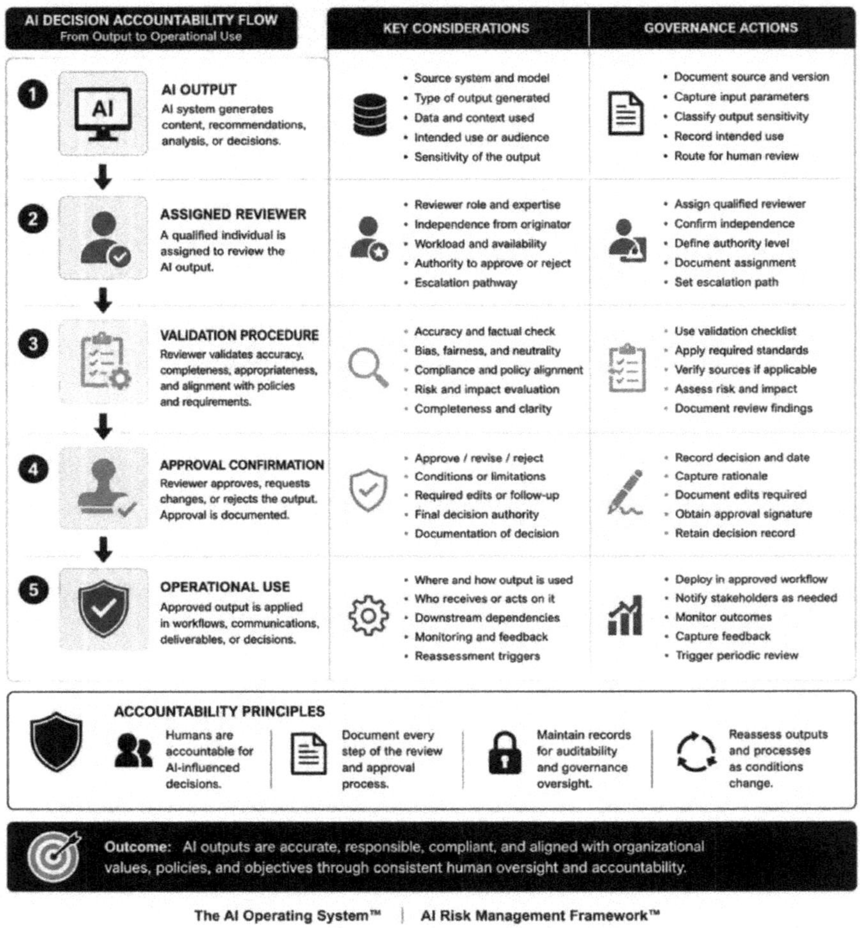

1. Assigned accountability ownership

Every consequential AI output has a named reviewer responsible for validating it before operational use. Not "someone in marketing." Not "the team will check it." A named individual or clearly defined role. Ambiguity at this layer is what produces governance failure later.

2. Defined validation procedures

The reviewer's job is specified, not implied. Examples: verify numerical accuracy; confirm alignment with source documentation; validate customer-specific information; review compliance-sensitive language; check operational assumptions; confirm consistency with brand or quality standards. The more clearly the review criteria are defined, the more dependable the process becomes.

3. Documented approval confirmation

Maintain traceable evidence that accountable review happened. Reviewer initials, workflow approval, document signoff, email confirmation, ticketing record. The point is not technical complexity — it is evidence that consequential outputs went through a defined review step before they affected the business.

The AI Oversight Log

For High-Accountability Systems, maintain a centralized oversight log capturing: date, AI system used, operational purpose, output description, assigned reviewer, approval confirmation. The log serves three governance purposes simultaneously — it documents that oversight occurred, creates traceability if a dispute or compliance question arises later, and surfaces governance patterns (if a specific system consistently produces outputs that require significant correction, that pattern is itself a signal worth acting on).

A practical accountability scenario

A mid-sized financial advisory firm uses an AI reporting platform to generate preliminary portfolio review summaries. The system saves real time. Over several months, reports begin flowing through the workflow with less human review the outputs have been acceptable, and the team's confidence in the platform has quietly grown. The firm has never written down who is responsible for validating financial assumptions, which calculations require verification, or what review standards must be met before external distribution. One quarter, the platform produces a confidently incorrect calculation in a client deliverable. The error is small in absolute terms. The compliance and reputational consequences are not. The fix was not better technology. The fix was a documented accountability framework that should have existed before the platform was operationally trusted.

Proportionate Mitigation Controls

Risk mitigation should be scaled to actual exposure. Applying enterprise-grade controls to every AI tool produces governance fatigue and gets ignored within a quarter. The three risk tiers from the assessment carry different control expectations.

Figure 7.5 — Proportionate Risk Mitigation Framework™

Apply mitigation controls that are appropriate to the level of AI risk exposure, ensuring effective governance without creating unnecessary operational burden.

High-risk systems — immediate action

For every High-Risk system, document: required governance controls, individual responsible for implementation, operational review owner, and implementation completion date. This documentation becomes the High-Risk Governance Action Plan. By exposure type:

Decision risk. AI Decision Accountability Framework™ controls (assigned reviewer, defined validation, documented approval).

Vendor dependency risk. Contingency framework (alternative vendor, transition timeline, manual workaround, accountability owner).

Compliance risk. Targeted governance review aligned to applicable regulatory, contractual, or privacy obligations. Where uncertainty exists about specific regulatory implications, narrowly-scoped consultation with appropriately qualified professionals is reasonable — the goal is operational clarity on defined exposure questions, not broad legal analysis.

Medium-risk systems — 60-day governance enhancement

Review vendor data-handling terms. Document operational usage expectations. Establish simplified oversight procedures. Create basic contingency documentation where dependency exists. Controls should be proportionate — meaningful but not enterprise-scale.

Low-risk systems — visibility and periodic review

Inventory documented. Included in recurring governance review. Additional controls are unnecessary unless usage materially changes, exposure categories expand, or vendor practices shift. The objective is to maintain visibility without unnecessary complexity.

Establishing a Governance Reassessment Schedule

Risk evolves. Usage patterns change. Vendor terms change. Integrations deepen. A governance framework built once and never revisited becomes obsolete the day organizational reality starts moving past it. Two reassessment mechanisms:

Figure 7.6 — Governance Reassessment & Oversight Cycle™

A continuous cycle for monitoring AI use, reassessing risk, and strengthening governance as tools, data, regulations, and organizational needs evolve.

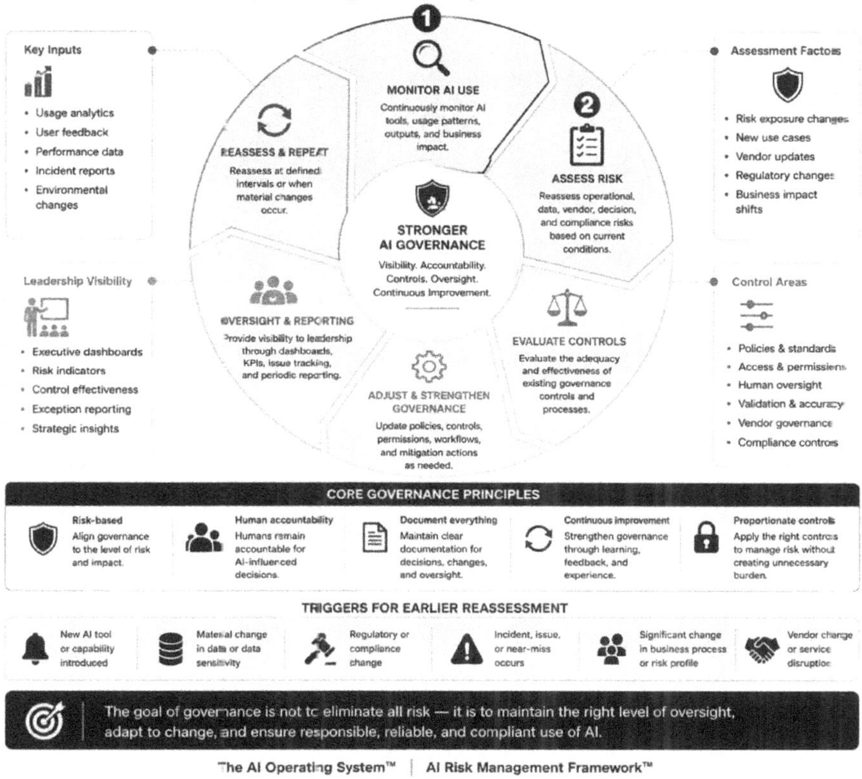

Scheduled annual reassessment. Every active AI system goes through formal reassessment during the annual governance review — risk classification, controls alignment, dependency exposure, and compliance posture.

Trigger-based reassessment. Immediate reassessment when vendor terms change materially, operational usage expands significantly, dependency exposure increases, pricing structures change, regulated data begins being processed, or the system becomes more operationally critical than originally intended (Hao et al., 2025).

From Exposure to Governance: Implementation Priorities

AI risk does not disappear through governance. It becomes manageable through it. The difference between a high-exposure company and a low-exposure company is rarely the technology stack. It is whether someone can answer, in a sentence, where the risk sits and who owns it.

Complete the following before moving to Chapter 8:

Within five business days — operational risk assessment. Run the ten-question assessment for every active AI system in the inventory. Assign Low, Medium, or High risk to each. Record classifications directly in the inventory.

Within ten business days — vendor dependency contingency plans. For every Tier 1 system carrying elevated vendor dependency, document the four contingency elements (alternative vendor, transition timeline, operational impact, accountability owner).

Within thirty days — decision accountability controls. Identify every High-Accountability AI System (client deliverables, employee decisions, financial outputs, operational recommendations, external communications). Implement the three Decision Accountability Framework controls — assigned reviewer, defined validation, documented approval.

Build the governance action plan. For every High-Risk system, document required controls, implementation ownership, completion deadline, and ongoing review owner. Establish 60-day enhancement plans for Medium-Risk systems. Schedule the annual reassessment. Document the trigger-based reassessment criteria.

When those controls are operational, AI risk stops being an undefined background concern and starts being a documented, classified, monitored, and governed operational discipline. The difference is not the absence of risk. The difference is the presence of governance.

Every AI-enabled system should undergo formal operational reassessment during the organization's annual AI governance review.

Chapter 8: AI Governance

Building the Rules That Keep Your Business Protected

CHAPTER OUTCOMES

At the end of this chapter, you will be able to:

- **Create a practical AI governance framework** that establishes accountability, approval standards, and operational oversight.
- **Build three core governance documents:** an AI Usage Policy, an AI Tool Approval Process, and a Data Access Protocol.
- **Define which AI systems, use cases, and data categories** are approved, restricted, or prohibited.
- **Implement a structured approval workflow** for evaluating and monitoring new AI tools.
- **Establish governance reinforcement mechanisms** that keep policies active, visible, and consistently followed.
- **Transform governance from a** compliance exercise into a competitive business advantage through clarity, trust, and operational discipline.

By this point in the framework, the business has visibility: an inventory of active tools, a documented cost picture, a performance baseline, and a risk assessment that classifies exposure by category and tier. Visibility is the prerequisite. It is not the destination.

Without governance, the same problems return. New tools enter without review. Employees make independent choices about which systems to use and what data to share with them. Costs creep upward. Risk drifts. The inventory built so carefully a quarter ago becomes inaccurate. The scorecards stop being run. The framework that produced visibility loses durability because there is no system maintaining it.

Governance is what makes the rest of the framework durable (Abonamah & Abdelhamid, 2024). It is the layer of rules, accountability, and approval discipline that lets AI oversight function without depending on constant leadership intervention. Done well, governance is what allows the company to adopt AI faster, not slower, because the operational questions have been settled in advance — what is permitted, who decides, what data is off-limits, where human review is required.

Governance is what keeps the AI Operating System™ durable, accountable, and aligned with the long-term success of the business.

I have spent most of my career watching organizations adopt technology faster than they could govern it, in accounting, in enterprise security, in operational consulting. The pattern always rhymes. Adoption races ahead. Governance lags. Then a client raises concern, a regulator asks a question, or an incident forces the issue, and leadership has to retrofit governance under duress. The companies that fared best in those situations were not the ones with the largest compliance departments. They were the ones that had written down the basics before the basics became urgent.

This chapter is about writing down the basics. By the end of it, the business will have three governance artifacts that together define how AI operates inside the company: an AI Usage Policy, an AI Tool Approval Process, and a Data Access Protocol. None of them requires a legal department. All of them are short, plain-language documents intended to be read, not filed.

What Governance Actually Means for Business

Governance is one of those words that gets in the way of itself. It sounds corporate, technical, and disconnected from a business trying to operate efficiently without standing up a compliance function. For that reason, many companies skip the conversation entirely and continue adopting AI tools informally, well past the point when every other consequential function in the business has developed some form of operating discipline around it.

In practice, AI governance reduces to three decisions:

- Who is authorized to use AI tools.
- Which tools are approved.
- What information those systems permit us to access.

When those boundaries are written down and consistently understood, AI usage becomes predictable. When they are not, employees make those judgment calls individually, and the cumulative result is shadow AI, unmanaged spend, inconsistent workflows, unreviewed outputs, and exposure leadership cannot see.

Every business already applies governance principles in other domains, regardless of whether the word "governance" appears in the conversation. Financial systems have access controls, not everyone can approve payments. Customer data is handled to documented standards even when the standards are informal. Hiring follows a workflow because inconsistent hiring is expensive. These structures exist because unrestricted access and inconsistent decisions produce real organizational cost. AI deserves the same treatment for the same reasons.

Governance is not bureaucracy. Bureaucracy is process for the sake of process. Governance is structure introduced because the absence of structure is more expensive than the structure itself. The test of any AI governance document is operational, not academic: can an employee answer the question "can I use this tool for this task?" in under thirty seconds without escalating?

Effective governance creates clarity, not friction. Employees should be able to tell quickly:

- Which AI systems are approved.
- Which use cases are permitted.
- Which data categories are restricted.
- When human review is required.
- Who to ask when they are not sure.

Three governance documents cover the entire space. Each one is short. Each one is operational. None of them requires a legal department to draft.

FIGURE 8.2

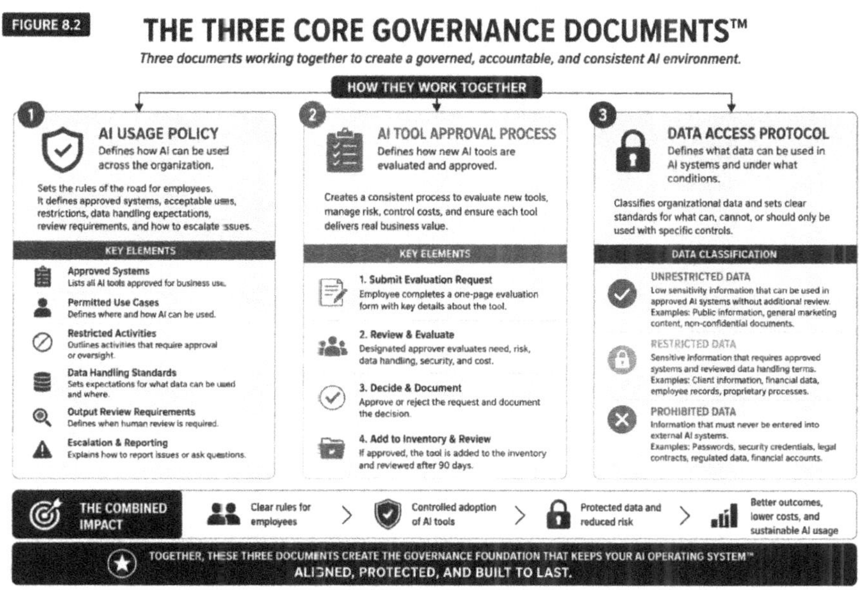

The Three Core Governance Documents Every Business Needs

Most governance frameworks fail because the documentation is too complicated to use in real operations (Sadiq et al., 2021). Companies draft long policies trying to cover every scenario, then discover that employees stop referencing them within weeks because the documents are hard to navigate and disconnect from daily work. The goal here is the opposite, concise, plain-language documents that can be read in minutes and applied without interpretation.

Document 1 — The AI Usage Policy

The Usage Policy is the foundational document. It establishes which AI systems are approved, how they may be used, what is restricted, and where human accountability is required. One to two pages. Plain language. Six sections:

Approved systems. The current list of authorized AI platforms. Use of any tool not on the list requires going through the approval process first. This closes the shadow AI loop directly.

Permitted use cases. Concrete categories where AI use is encouraged, drafting internal communications, generating first drafts for review, summarizing meetings, automating repetitive formatting, researching publicly available information. Specific, not abstract.

Restricted activities. Activities requiring additional approval or structured human review, sending client communications without review, processing personally identifiable information through unapproved systems, generating financial reports without verification, making employment decisions on AI outputs alone.

Data handling expectations. Everyday translation of the Data Access Protocol. Which information may be used freely, which requires approved systems, which is prohibited entirely.

Output review requirements. Which categories of AI output require documented human review before use or distribution. Client deliverables, financial outputs, HR documentation, legal communications, and outputs from High-Accountability systems from Chapter 7.

Reporting and escalation. How to request approval for new tools, where to ask governance questions, how to report concerns. Clear escalation paths reduce judgment-call governance and surface issues early.

If the Usage Policy runs longer than two pages, it is doing something the document is not supposed to do. The whole point is that an employee can read it on the first day and refer back to it without effort.

FIGURE 8.3

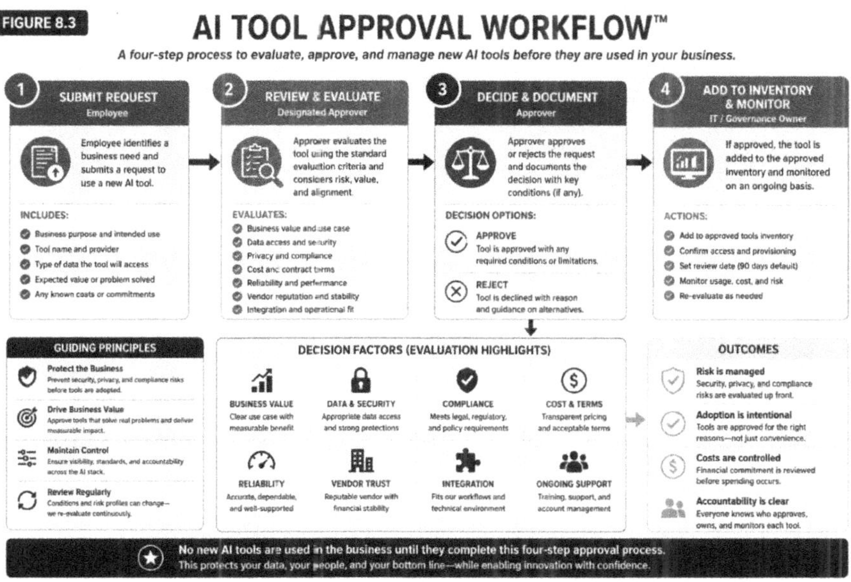

Document 2 — The AI Tool Approval Process

The Approval Process governs how new AI systems enter the company. Its job is to prevent the patterns from Chapters 2 through 5, informal vendor adoption, unmanaged subscription growth, duplicate functionality, unreviewed data exposure, by making sure every new tool clears a simple, consistent review before it touches business data.

A four-step workflow that takes under thirty minutes per request:

Standardized request. The employee proposing the tool completes a one-page form: tool name, vendor, problem being solved, estimated cost, data exposure, whether an approved alternative already exists.

Designated approver. The request routes to a named governance owner, ownership, operations, IT, or a designated governance manager, depending on the size of the company. One name per role, not a committee.

Four-question evaluation. Does the tool solve a real operational need? Does expected value justify cost? Are vendor data-handling terms acceptable? Does the system meet minimum security standards?

Decision + inventory entry. Approved systems get added to the inventory with a 90-day performance review date scheduled. Rejected requests receive a brief written explanation, credibility depends on consistency and transparency.

Approval should be fast for low-risk tools and deliberate for high-risk ones. The point is not gatekeeping; it is governance visibility before dependency forms.

FIGURE 8.4 **AI DATA ACCESS CLASSIFICATION MODEL™**

Three data categories. Clear rules for what can, cannot, or should only be used with specific controls.

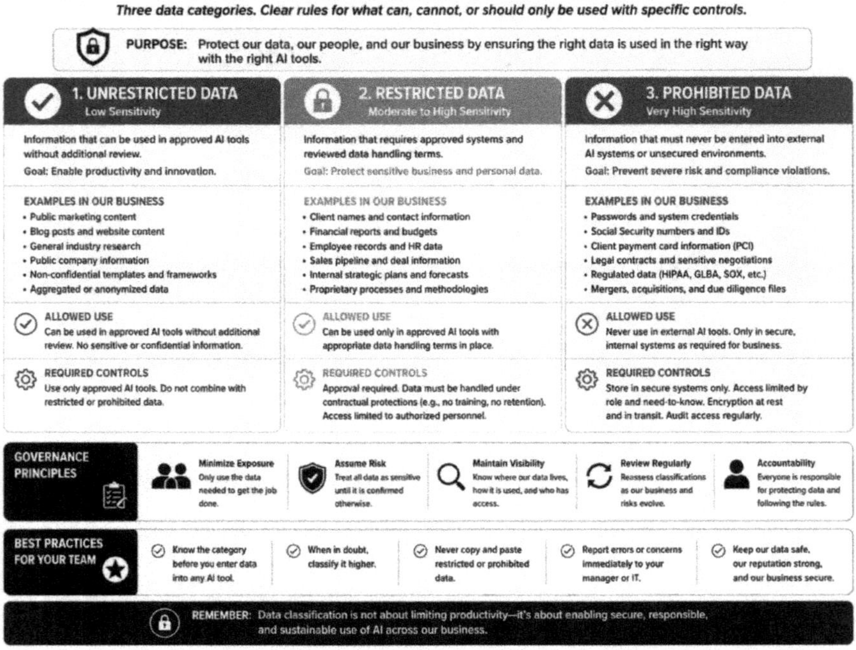

Document 3 — The Data Access Protocol

The Data Access Protocol defines what information may be entered into AI systems, under what conditions. Three categories, with specific examples drawn from the company's own operations:

Table 8.1 — The three-category Data Access Protocol

The Protocol also requires that vendor privacy policies, retention practices, data storage location, and model training disclosures be reviewed before any system is approved to process Restricted data (Pumplun et al., 2019). Decisions about data are informed decisions, not assumptions about vendor practices.

Together the three documents define how AI operates: who, what, where, with what data, under what review. They do not require a compliance department. They require clarity, consistency, and the discipline to write things down before complexity arrives.

Getting Your Team to Actually Follow the Policies

A governance policy that lives in a shared folder and is not governance. It is the appearance of governance, which is more dangerous than no governance at all, it creates the impression that exposure is managed while the actual behavior remains unchanged.

Adoption is a design problem before it is a communication problem. Policies get followed when they are easy to understand, easy to find, and easy to act on. They get ignored when they are buried, written in language requiring interpretation, or structured so the compliant path takes more effort than the workaround. The goal is to make following the policies the path of least resistance.

The thirty-minute rollout meeting

Start with one short meeting. Thirty minutes. Not a line-by-line policy walk-through; that is the wrong format. The purpose is to explain why the framework exists, what it covers at a high level, where the documents live, and what to do when an employee runs into a situation where the documents do not clearly address.

First five minutes — the why. Unmanaged AI creates real cost and real risk. Clear rules protect the business and the people working in it. Not a response to anyone doing anything wrong, a natural step in building a company that uses AI responsibly.

Next fifteen minutes — the three documents at summary level. Do not read them aloud. Two or three sentences per section. Ask for questions before moving on. Use concrete examples from your own operations rather than abstract scenarios, they land better.

Last ten minutes — questions and access. Make sure everyone knows where the documents are stored and where the request forms live. Put the links in the team's existing communication channel, the shared drive, and wherever the team already goes for internal reference.

Within twenty-four hours of the meeting, send a written summary. One paragraph. What the framework covers, where to find the documents, who to contact with questions. This becomes the reference point for the conversation and lets anyone who missed the meeting catch up.

Three lightweight reinforcement mechanisms

The rollout is the starting point, not the end point. Policies stick when they are reinforced through normal operations rather than introduced once and abandoned.

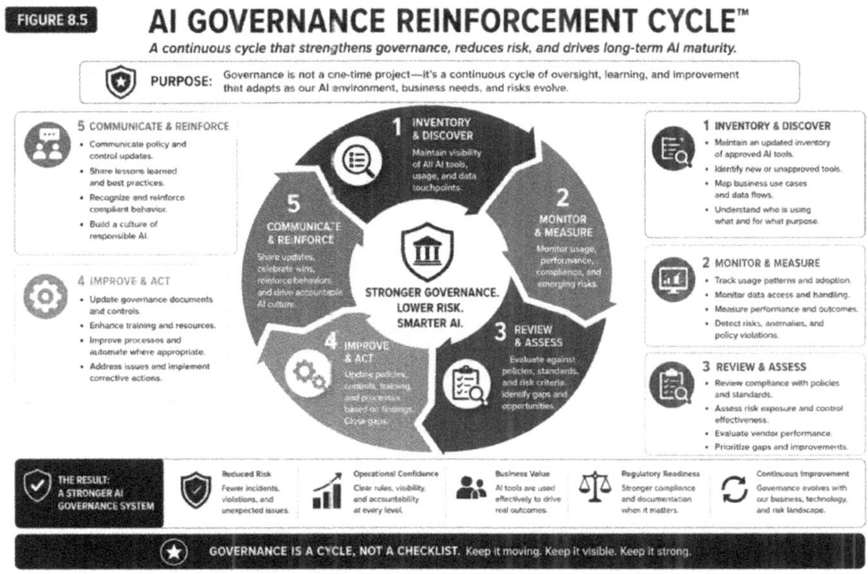

Monthly check-in. Add one question to the monthly inventory review: has anything come up this month where the governance policies were unclear or hard to follow? This signals the policies are active and surfaces gaps in the documents, if the same situation keeps coming up as a gray area, that is a signal to revise the document, not to expect the team to keep navigating the ambiguity.

Onboarding acknowledgment. New hires and contractors receive the three documents as part of onboarding and sign a brief acknowledgment that they have read and understood the Usage Policy. Not a legal document. A one-line email confirmation is enough. The point is that the policy is part of how people are introduced to the company, not something they discover six months in when a situation comes up.

Quarterly governance review. Spend ten minutes during the quarterly audit checking whether the three documents are still accurate. Has the approved tool list changed? Have data-handling rules evolved as new tools or new vendor terms came in? Have restricted use cases come up that need to be added? Documents that have drifted from reality get ignored.

Handling pushback

Some employees will push back on governance, not because they have bad intentions, but because structure feels like constraint. The most effective response is not to defend the policies. It is to connect the policies to outcomes the person already cares about (Dey et al., 2023). Someone frustrated by the Approval Process cares about doing their job efficiently, explain how the process prevents them from spending two months on a tool that turns out to be a compliance risk or a cost line that gets cut on the next review. Someone frustrated by the Data Access Protocol cares about doing their work well — explain how the protocol protects them from inadvertently sharing client data with a vendor whose terms are problematic. Governance connected to outcomes people care about stops feeling like constraint and starts feeling like support.

FIGURE 8.6

The goal is not perfect compliance enforced through surveillance. The goal is a team that understands the rules well enough to follow them naturally, because the rules make sense and the purpose behind them is clear. That understanding does not come from a policy document. It comes from a clear introduction, consistent reinforcement, and a governance structure designed to be easy to follow rather than easy to circumvent (Alzahrani, 2025).

Putting It into Practice

Governance is what makes everything else in The AI Operating System™ durable. Without it, inventories drift out of date, costs creep upward, risk exposure expands as new tools enter informally, and the discipline that produced the initial visibility quietly fades (Westover, 2025). The three-week implementation sequence:

Week 1 — Draft the three governance documents. Build the AI Usage Policy using the six-section structure above — one to two pages, plain language. Build the AI Tool Approval Process workflow and the accompanying one-page evaluation form. Build the Data Access Protocol using the three-category structure, populating each category with examples drawn from the company's actual operations rather than generic templates. Store all three in a shared location accessible without special permission.

Week 2 — Run the rollout meeting and start the acknowledgment process. Hold the thirty-minute governance introduction meeting using the structure above. Send the one-paragraph written summary within twenty-four hours. Add the governance acknowledgment to onboarding for new hires and contractors.

Week 3 — Integrate governance into the recurring rhythm. Add the one-question governance check to the monthly inventory review. Schedule the first quarterly governance document review approximately ninety days out. Confirm the documents remain current as approved tools, data handling rules, and use cases evolve.

When those three weeks are complete, governance is no longer a document folder. It is part of how the business operates. AI usage functions inside defined standards. Approval is structured. Data handling is documented. The team understands what is expected, leadership keeps visibility into how AI is being used, and the framework has a maintenance mechanism that keeps it accurate as adoption expands.

That is what real AI governance looks like in a working business, Governance is what makes the rest of the framework durable (Abonamah & Abdelhamid, 2024). It is the layer of rules, accountability, and approval discipline that lets AI oversight function without depending on constant leadership intervention, not a perfect system, but a documented, maintained, consistently applied one. Enough structure to keep the company operating with clarity, accountability, and discipline as AI becomes increasingly integrated into how the work gets done.

Chapter 9: Aligning AI With Business Goals

Making Every Tool Earn Its Place

CHAPTER OUTCOMES

At the end of this chapter, you will be able to:

- **Build the AI-to-Outcome Alignment Map™** for every active AI system in your inventory using five simple columns.
- **Define specific business objectives** and supporting metrics that tie each AI system to measurable results.
- **Evaluate current performance** and classify each system as Aligned, Partial, or Unaligned.
- **Identify misaligned AI activity** and make clear decisions to optimize, realign, or retire systems.
- **Assign clear ownership and accountability** for outcomes, metrics, and ongoing AI performance.
- **Ensure every AI investment earns its place** by connecting AI activity to business goals that drive measurable growth.

The Alignment Problem — When AI Activity Doesn't Connect to Business Outcomes

Inside many companies, AI is producing activity without producing results. Content goes out faster. Workflows run more smoothly. Reports generate themselves. Employees look measurably more productive. Yet when leadership looks at the metrics the business actually cares about — revenue, margin, retention, customer acquisition — the needles have not moved.

That gap is the most common AI governance failure in the market right now (Sadiq et al., 2021). It is also one of the hardest to see, because everything looks busy. The dashboards are alive. The tools are running. Adoption charts trend up. But the business outcomes the company actually exists to produce, revenue, profitability, retention, strategic execution, remain disconnected from the systems consuming the budget.

Three patterns worth recognizing

The misalignment usually shows up as one of three patterns:

Volume without conversion. A marketing AI generates four times the content. Lead quality and customer acquisition are unchanged. The system is doing exactly what it was designed to do, but the design was not tied to the metric that matters.

Automation without acceleration. Reporting workflows get automated. Administrative tasks get handled. Decision-making speed and operational accuracy do not improve, because the bottleneck was never the report — it was the review cycle that comes after.

Productivity without effectiveness. Multiple productivity platforms are adopted simultaneously. Employees report saving hours. Profitability, retention, and strategic execution remain flat. The hours saved are real; they just are not being redeployed to anything that produces measurable business value.

In all three cases, the technology is working as designed. The alignment is what is missing. The system was adopted because it looked useful, not because someone defined which business objective it was supposed to support, what measurable outcome it would improve, or how success would be evaluated.

Speed is not a strategy. Automation is not improvement. Volume is not value. AI creates business impact only when operational activity is intentionally aligned to measurable organizational objectives, with clear accountability and recurring performance evaluation. The previous chapters built the foundation: visibility, cost, performance, risk, and governance. This chapter adds the strategic alignment layer, making sure every active AI system supports a defined business objective and produces a measurable result against it (Westover, 2025).

By the end of the chapter, the company will be able to point at every active AI system in the inventory and answer four questions in a sentence each: what business objective it supports, what metric measures that support, what the current performance is, and whether the system is aligned, partially aligned, or unaligned. Systems that cannot answer those four questions in plain language are not strategic AI investments. They are AI activities dressed up as strategy.

The AI-to-Outcome Alignment Map™

The AI-to-Outcome Alignment Map™ is the artifact that closes the gap. One row per active system. Five columns. Built directly on top of the inventory from Chapter 4.

Tool Name	Business Objective	Supporting Metric	Current Performance	Alignment Status
AI Content Platform	Increase qualified inbound leads 20% within 2 quarters	Monthly qualified inquiries	+8% over baseline	Partial
AI Reporting Assistant	Reduce monthly financial reporting prep time by 50%	Hours of prep per close cycle	−42%	Aligned
AI Meeting Notes	Improve cross-team handoff quality	Handoff-error rate per project	Not tracked	Unaligned

Table 9.1 — AI-to-Outcome Alignment Map: sample rows

Building the five columns

Tool name. Every active AI system from the inventory. Exercise is exhaustive; inactive or already-retired tools do not belong on the map.

Business objective. Not a description of what technology does. The specific organizational outcome the system is expected to have. The objective belongs to one of four broad categories, revenue growth, cost reduction, operational efficiency, customer experience, but the entry needs to be specific. "Improving marketing" is not an objective. "Increase qualified inbound leads from content marketing by 20% within two quarters" is. "Reduce administrative burden" is not an objective. "Reduce monthly financial reporting preparation time by 50%" is. The more specific the objective, the easier the system is to evaluate.

Supporting metric. The measurable indicator that demonstrates whether the objective is being achieved (Soomro et al., 2025). Qualified inquiries. Hours per close cycle. Customer-response time. Error rate. If the metric is hard to identify, the objective is probably still too vague, tighten it.

Current performance. What the metric shows. A blank field is more useful than an estimate; it tells leadership which systems lack measurement infrastructure entirely. Often the act of populating this column is when companies discover that performance claims they had treated as facts were assumptions.

Alignment status. Three classifications:

Aligned — clearly defined objective + measurable metric + evidence the metric is moving in the intended direction.

Partial — some connection to an objective, but missing performance data, inconsistent tracking, or inconclusive results.

Unaligned — cannot be tied to a clear business objective or fails to show meaningful contribution despite extended use.

Once classified, leadership has, for the first time, visibility into whether the company's AI stack is strategically aligned or merely operationally active. A stack where most systems are Aligned indicates disciplined governance and strategic adoption. A stack where large portions are Partial or Unaligned signals reactive adoption running ahead of the business priorities the tools were supposed to support.

FIGURE 9.1 **AI Alignment Status Framework™**

Use this framework to assess and manage the alignment status of every AI tool in your stack.

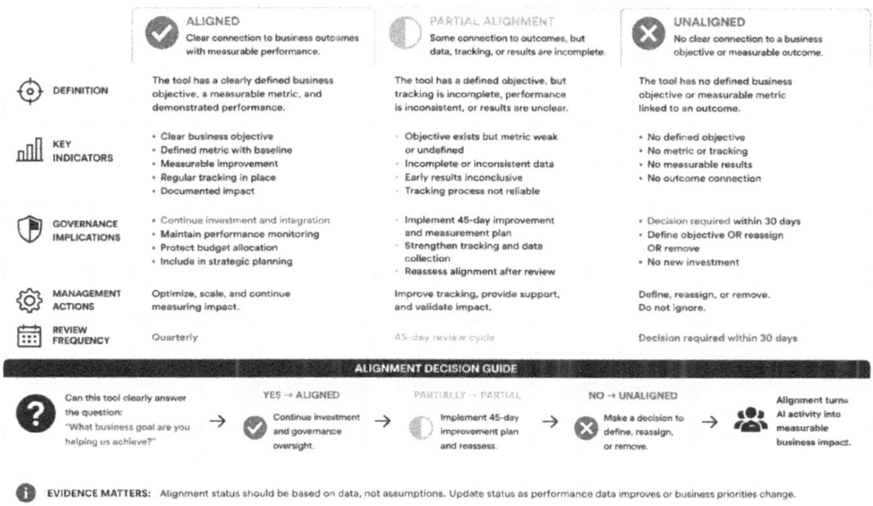

What to do with each classification

Aligned. Maintain. Continue performance review and optimization. These systems are doing what they were adopted to do.

Partial. Structured improvement plan. Clarify the objective. Strengthen metric tracking. Set a defined review window (typically 60–90 days) and reclassify after.

Unaligned. Immediate reassessment. Leadership must either establish measurable alignment or transition the system out of the environment. The principle is decisiveness, a documented decision, even one that gets adjusted later, is operationally stronger than indefinite inaction (Abonamah & Abdelhamid, 2024).

The Alignment Map also operates as a forward governance mechanism. Before any new AI tool clears the approval process from Chapter 8, it should require a completed Alignment Map entry, proposed business objective, supporting metric, expected performance outcome. If those fields cannot be filled in clearly before adoption, the tool does not get approved. That single requirement prevents a meaningful percentage of misaligned spending before dependency forms.

Prioritizing AI Investments Based on Strategic Impact

Alignment classifies systems by whether they support a business objective. Prioritization classifies them by how much organizational investment, governance attention, and operational protection each deserves.

Not every aligned system is equally important. A system aligned to a mission-critical revenue objective is not the same as a system aligned to a peripheral administrative convenience. The prioritization framework evaluates each system on two dimensions:

Strategic impact. How directly does the system contributes to the company's most important business goals. High / Medium / Low.

Operational dependency. How deeply embedded the system is in core workflows. Uses the same Tier 1 / Tier 2 / Tier 3 structure from Chapter 4 (Alzahrani, 2025).

Together, the two dimensions produce a 2×2 grid with four quadrants. Each quadrant calls for a different governance posture.

FIGURE 9.2 **Strategic Impact vs Operational Dependency Matrix™**

Use this matrix to prioritize AI investments, allocate governance attention, and determine the right management approach for every tool in your stack.

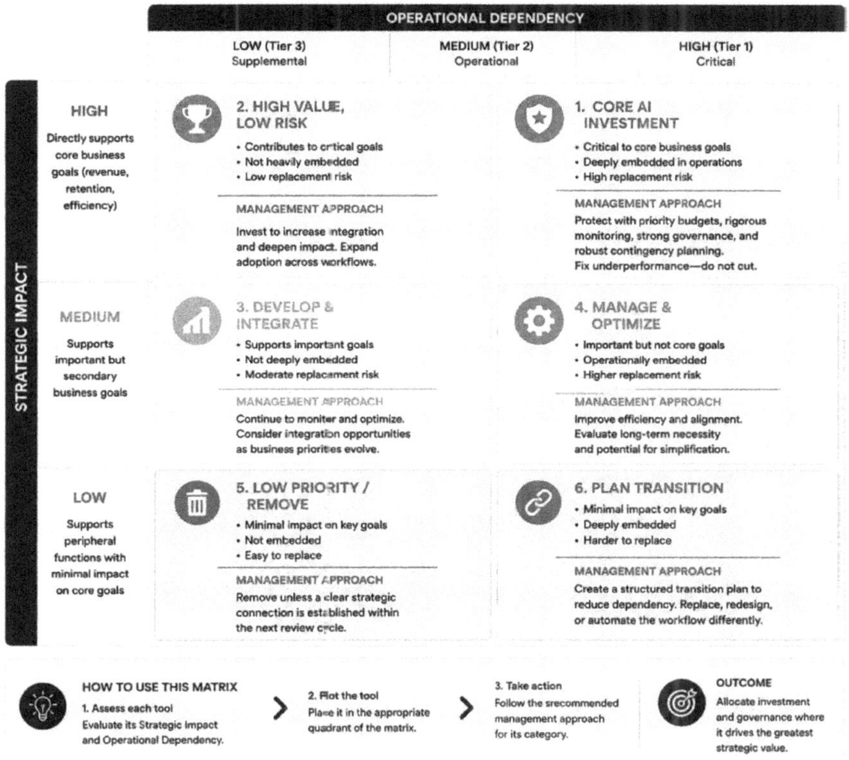

The four quadrants

Core — High Impact / High Dependency. The company's foundational AI investments. Essential business objective + deep operational embedding. Highest governance oversight, most protected budget, strongest contingency planning. When these systems underperform, optimizing before replacing, disruption cost is usually higher than improvement cost. Failures in this quadrant cascade across multiple business functions, so the controls must match.

Underutilized — High Impact / Low Dependency. Strategically valuable systems that have not yet been integrated deeply. One of the most common findings during the exercise, leadership often finds tools for doing meaningful work for a single team or workflow that could be extended across the company. The right response is usually expansion, not maintenance.

Problems: Low Impact / High Dependency. The most difficult governance situation in the AI environment. Operational reliance has formed around a system that does not contribute to strategic priorities. Employees depend on it; leadership cannot defend it. Immediate removal would create workflow instability. Structured transition planning, gradual dependency reduction, workflow redesign, or replacement with a more aligned system, is the right play.

Peripheral — Low Impact / Low Dependency. The simplest governance decisions. Limited strategic value, easy to remove. Unless a meaningful purpose can be established inside a defined review period, these systems are candidates for retirement. Every Peripheral system consumes governance attention that could go to a Core or Underutilized one.

Once every system has been classified, the company has a prioritized AI investment hierarchy: Core gets protected, Underutilized gets expanded, Problematic gets transition-planned, Peripheral gets reassessed or removed. The hierarchy directly informs the budget framework from Chapter 5, the governance controls from Chapter 8, and every future adoption decision. AI stops being distributed evenly across systems of radically different strategic value.

Once systems are classified by strategic importance and dependency, leadership must determine how investment, governance attention, and operational resources should be allocated across the portfolio.

FIGURE 9.3 **AI Investment Prioritization Hierarchy™**

Use this hierarchy to determine where to invest, what to improve, and what to transition or remove.

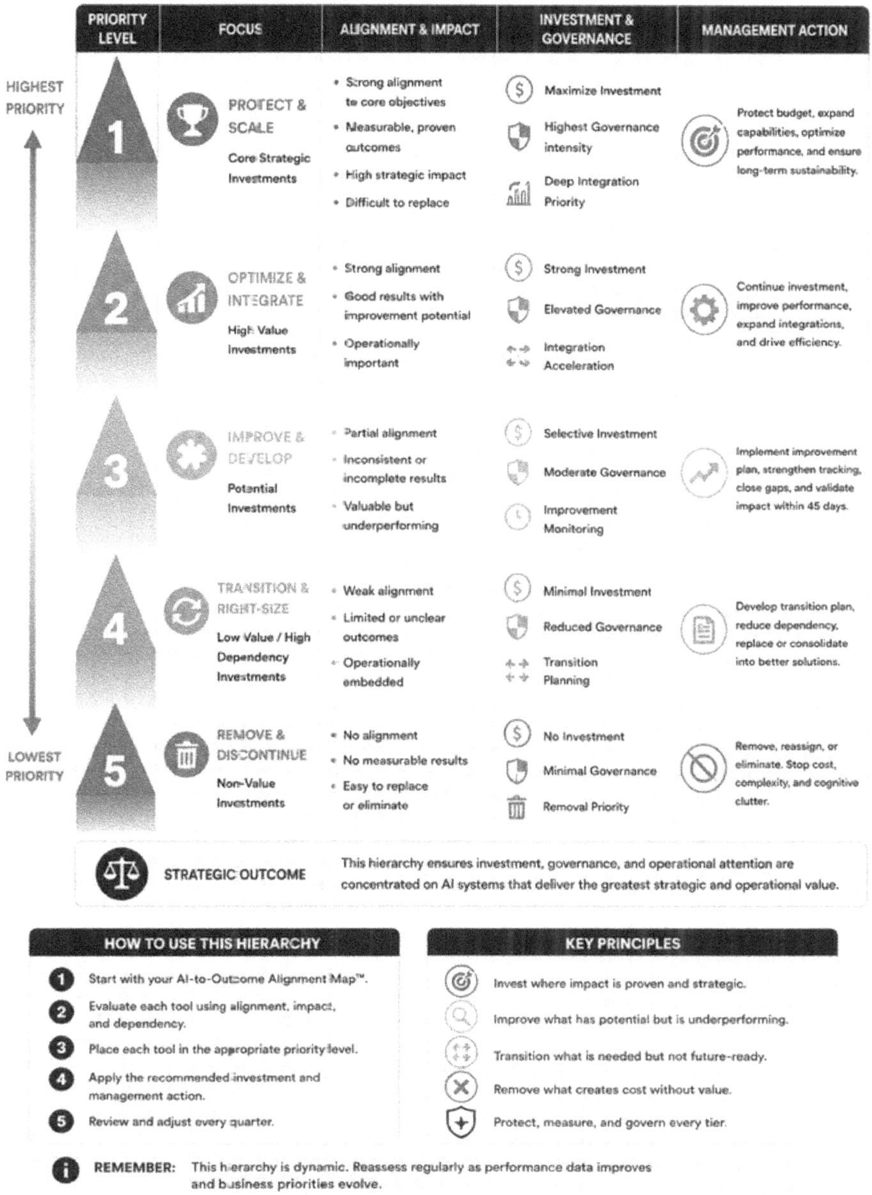

The framework gets re-run during the quarterly governance review. Business priorities shift over time. Objectives that were central two quarters ago may have softened. Strategic impact ratings need to evolve alongside the business they are measuring. A static prioritization carried forward unchanged is the same governance failure as no prioritization at all.

FIGURE 9.4 Preventative AI Alignment Governance Cycle™

A continuous cycle to ensure every AI system remains aligned, measurable, and valuable over time.

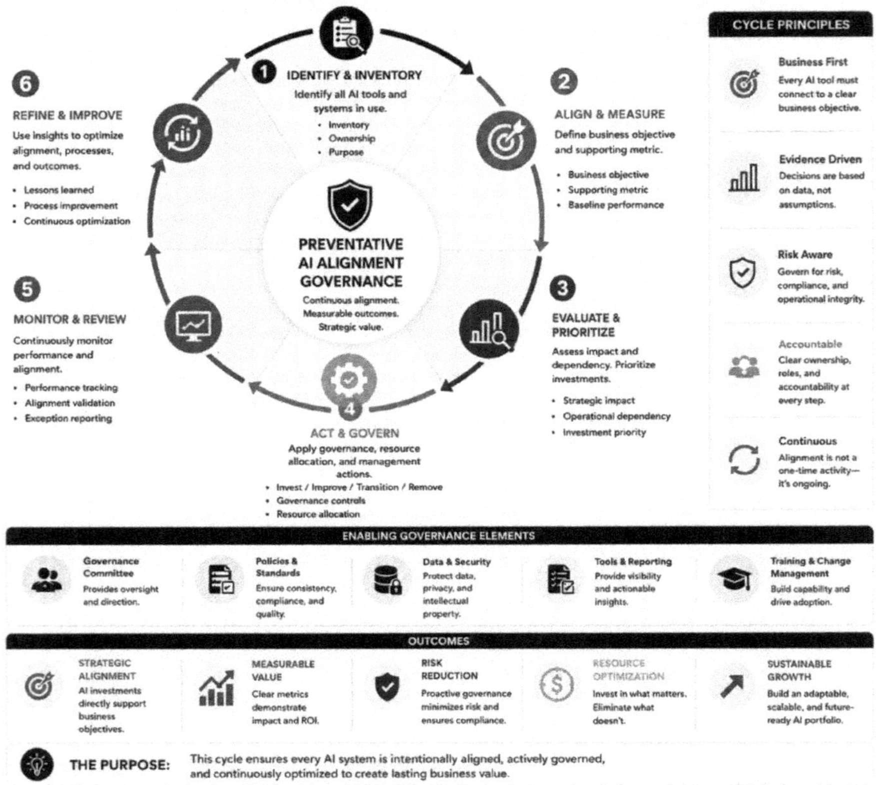

Your Next Move

Every active AI system in the company should be able to answer one question in a sentence: what measurable business objective is this system helping achieve? Systems that cannot answer that question clearly are not strategically aligned, regardless of how active, popular, or impressive they look operationally.

The five implementation priorities for this chapter:

1. Build the Alignment Map. Five columns, every active system. Tool name, business objective, supporting metric, current performance, alignment status. Where leadership cannot define a clear objective, classify the system Unaligned, do not retroactively invent justifications for systems whose value cannot be explained concretely.

2. Address every Unaligned system inside thirty days. Three options per system: define a legitimate measurable objective and put the system on a structured review period, reassign the system to a function where alignment can be established, or remove it. A documented decision, even one adjusted later, is operationally stronger than indefinite inaction.

3. Run the Prioritization Framework. Evaluate every system on strategic impact and operational dependency. Place each in one of the four quadrants. Document the governance response per quadrant (protect, expand, transition, remove). Each action gets an owner and a deadline — frameworks without accountability are documentation, not governance.

4. Integrate alignment into the Approval Process from Chapter 8. No new AI tool clears approval without a completed Alignment Map entry: proposed objective, supporting metric, expected performance outcome. Alignment before adoption is dramatically more effective than alignment after dependency. This single requirement prevents a meaningful share of the next twelve months of misaligned spending.

5. Quarterly alignment review. The Alignment Map and Prioritization Framework get refreshed every quarter inside the existing governance cycle. Update performance, reassess alignment, refresh strategic impact ratings, confirm whether business priorities themselves have moved.

When those five priorities are complete, the company has something most businesses never establish formally, a documented strategic rationale for every AI system operating inside it. Leadership can name, in one sentence per system, what it supports, how success is measured, where current performance sits, and why the company continues investing in it. That clarity converts AI from operational activity into measurable strategic investment.

Chapter 10: Operational Integration & Workflow Adoption

CHAPTER OUTCOMES

At the end of this chapter, you will be able to:

- **Identify** why AI tools fail at the integration level despite strong technology.
- **Use the AI Integration Checklist™** to embed AI into recurring operational workflows.
- **Design workflow triggers,** ownership, review controls, and measurable outputs for AI systems.
- **Standardize AI usage** across departments to improve consistency and operational performance.
- **Conduct 30-day Operational Health Check™** reviews to validate adoption and workflow execution.
- **Transform AI systems** from optional tools into embedded operational infrastructure.

Making AI Function Inside the Business, Not Beside It

By this point in the framework, the company has done substantial governance work. AI is inventoried, costed, performance-evaluated, risk-assessed, governed by written policy, and aligned to measurable business objectives. That alone puts the business ahead of most companies adopting AI right now.

And the work is not yet finished.

An AI system can be approved, budgeted, governed, aligned, and monitored — and still produce no reliable organizational value if it was never built into how the work actually gets done. Value does not emerge from having a tool. Value emerges when the tool becomes operationally integrated into recurring workflows — embedded in daily execution, not optional alongside it (Westover, 2025).

The pattern is recognizable. Employees use the system occasionally. Different departments develop different usage patterns. Some workflows lean on AI heavily; others ignore it. Leadership assumes integration exists because the tool was introduced. Actual adoption is fragmented, inconsistent, and dependent on individual initiative. The result is uneven operational outcomes, unpredictable workflow behavior, duplicated manual work, and unreliable performance improvement (Sánchez et al., 2025).

The technology is usually working as designed. Integration is what is missing. The system remains adjacent to the workflow rather than embedded inside it, and the difference between those two conditions is what determines whether AI produces business results.

A system employees *can use* is fundamentally different from a system employees *operationally rely on* as part of standardized workflow execution. Optional usage produces inconsistent outcomes. Integrated usage produces repeatable performance. This chapter is about closing that gap.

Three layers, working together:

Governance establishes the rules.

Alignment establishes the purpose.

Integration establishes the execution (Alzahrani, 2025).

Figure 10.1 — Workflow Integration Transformation™

From Optional AI Usage to Embedded Operational Execution

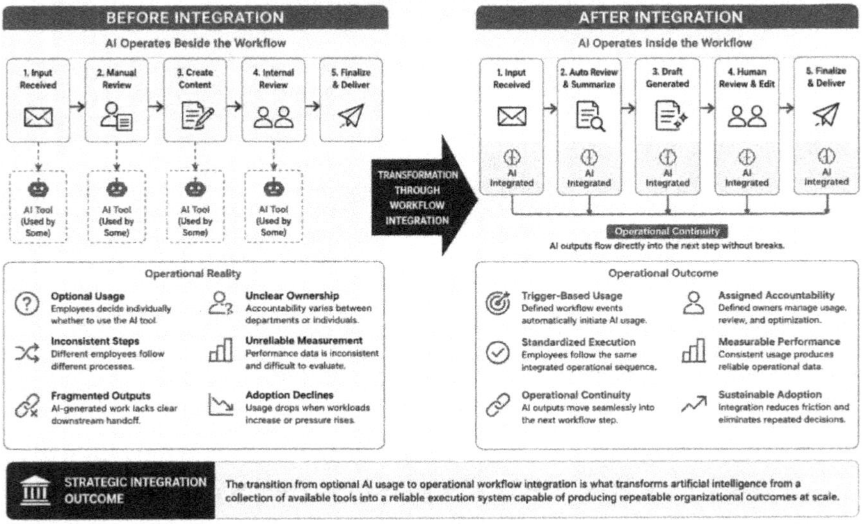

When all three operate together, AI stops being an isolated collection of tools and starts being embedded in operational infrastructure capable of producing consistent, measurable business outcomes at scale.

Why AI Tools Fail at the Integration Level

Most AI tools do not fail because the technology does not work. They fail because they were never built into the workflows they were supposed to support. The tool exists. The subscription is active. The team knows it is available. Using it is optional, inconsistent, and dependent on individual initiative rather than building into how the work actually gets done.

That is the integration gap, and it is the most common AI implementation failure in the market right now.

The pattern is recognizable in practice. A company adopts an AI tool to improve the speed and quality of client proposals. The tool is approved, the team gets a brief introduction, everyone agrees it sounds promising. For the first two weeks, adoption is strong — outputs look good, momentum is real. By week six, usage had dropped to about half the team. By week twelve, two people use it consistently, three use it occasionally, and the rest have drifted back to the old process. The subscription is still running. The impact that looked promising in week two has quietly evaporated, because nobody built the tool into the actual step-by-step process for creating a proposal. It was introduced as an option, not embedded as a step.

That is not a problem with people. It is a workflow design problem.

When a tool is introduced without being connected to a specific step in a specific workflow, adoption depends entirely on individual habit formation. Some people form the habit. Most do not, especially under pressure on time or in unfamiliar situations where the old approach feels safer and faster. Human behavior defaults to the familiar when friction is present, and a tool that is not built into the workflow creates friction every time someone has to decide whether to use it.

There is a second consequence that does not get enough attention. When AI tools sit alongside workflows rather than inside them, the company loses the ability to measure their impact reliably. If some people use the tool and some do not, performance data is contaminated. The company cannot tell whether the results it sees come from the tool or from the people who happen to use it. Configuration cannot be improved because outputs cannot be attributed cleanly. Decisions to keep, expand, or replace the tool cannot be made confidently because usage is too inconsistent to produce usable data.

Consistent usage produce's consistent data. Consistent data makes every other piece of this management system accurate. Without it, performance scores are unreliable, ROI calculations are estimates at best, and the Alignment Map operates on partial information. Integration is what makes the rest of the framework work.

The fix is not more training or encouragement. The fix is workflow design. When a tool is built into the process at a specific step, with a specific trigger that initiates its use and a specific output that moves the work forward, usage becomes automatic rather than optional. The decision to use the tool stops being a daily choice and becomes a built-in part of how the task gets done. That is the standard the rest of this chapter is designed to install.

The AI Integration Checklist™ — Embedding Tools That Actually Stick

Figure 10.2 — AI Integration Checklist™

Seven Decisions That Must Be Made Before Any Tool Goes Live in a Workflow

#	INTEGRATION QUESTION	WHAT TO DEFINE	EXAMPLE (PROPOSAL WORKFLOW)	KEY OUTCOME
1	Which specific workflow does this tool belong in, and at which step?	• Workflow name • Exact step number • Clear integration point	*"Proposal Creation Workflow, Step 5: Prepare kickoff call agenda based on questionnaire responses."*	Tool has a precise home in the workflow.
2	What specific task within that step will the tool handle?	• Task description • Type of output (draft, summary, extraction, analysis, etc.)	*"Generate first draft of agenda using client responses and key project information."*	Everyone understands the tool's operational responsibility.
3	What is the trigger that initiates the tool's use?	• Event or condition • Specific trigger point	*"When the completed questionnaire is received and all required fields are submitted."*	Tool usage becomes automatic, not optional.
4	What does the output of the tool look like, and what happens to it next?	• Expected output • Format or destination • Next step / handoff	*"Draft agenda in Google Doc. Next step: 5-minute human review before sending to client."*	Outputs flow forward with operational continuity.
5	Who is responsible for using this tool at this step?	• Named individual or role • Accountability for correct use	*"Account Coordinator (Primary Owner)."*	Clear accountability and ownership.
6	What is the review requirement for this tool's output?	• Review level (none, self-check, peer review, approve) • Reviewer (if applicable)	*"Self-check by Account Coordinator. Peer review by Project Manager for final approval."*	Quality and risk are managed consistently.
7	How will you measure whether this integration is working?	• Specific metric • Target and baseline • Review date	*Metric: Time spent on agenda preparation. Target: Reduce from 45 min to 20 min. Review Date: 30 days post-go-live."*	Success is measurable and tied to business outcomes.

HOW TO USE THIS CHECKLIST

- Complete all seven questions for every tool-workflow-step combination BEFORE the tool goes live.
- If any answer is unclear, the integration is not ready—resolve the gap before deployment.
- Store the completed checklist as the integration record in your tool inventory.

A well-designed integration today prevents inconsistent usage, workflow friction, and wasted investment tomorrow.

Integration does not happen by default. It requires deliberate operational decisions before a tool enters a workflow. When those decisions are not made up front, the tool is used inconsistently, used incorrectly, or ignored entirely once initial enthusiasm fades. The AI Integration Checklist™ closes that gap by requiring every integration to be designed before the system goes live.

Seven questions. The answers define how the tool will be used, who will use it, what output it should produce, what review is required, and how success will be measured.

The checklist applies in two situations: new tools entering through the approval process from Chapter 8, and existing tools already active but inconsistently used. If a tool is available but usage varies by employee, department, or situation, the tool has not been fully integrated. It may be approved, budgeted, and aligned, but it is still operating beside the workflow rather than inside it.

Table 10.1 — The AI Integration Checklist (seven operational design questions)

Each answer matters for a specific reason. Question 1 forces workflow-step specificity, without it, integration becomes vague guidance rather than a defined operational change. Question 3 (the trigger) is one of the most important controls in the entire framework, because it removes the daily decision about whether to use the tool and turns usage into a built-in workflow step. Questions 4 and 5 prevent outputs from sitting outside the workflow with no clear path forward. Question 6 connects review expectations to the Decision Accountability Framework from Chapter 7 (Yablonsky, 2021; Heger et al., 2025). Question 7 ties the integration to a measurable success criterion so leadership knows whether the change is producing the intended result.

Figure 10.3 — AI Workflow Trigger & Handoff Model™

From Trigger to Operational Continuity

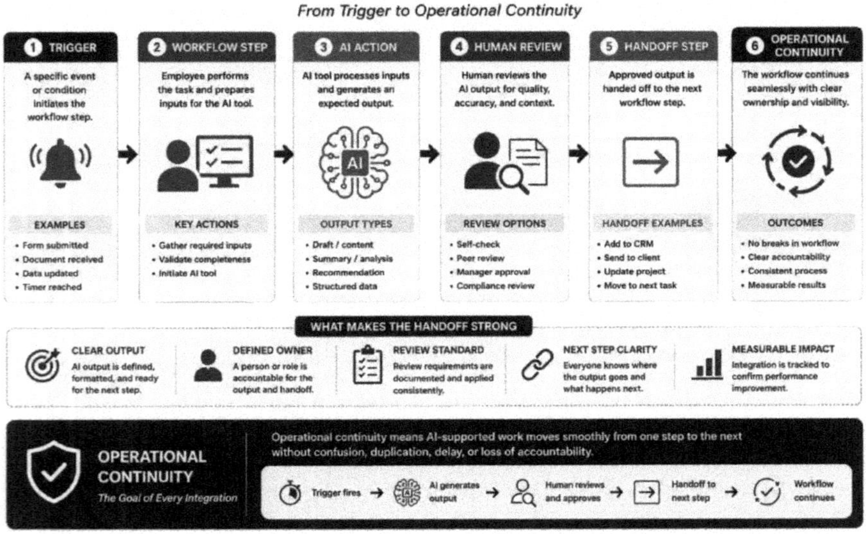

Strong triggers matter especially. Recent operational integration research has reinforced that adoption consistency depends almost entirely on whether the workflow itself initiates system usage, rather than the employee deciding situationally each time (Hao et al., 2025).

The integration record

The seven answers get documented in an integration record stored alongside the tool's inventory entry, governance documentation, performance scorecard, and alignment record. During monthly check-ins and quarterly reviews, leadership uses the integration record to confirm the tool is being used as designed and the performance metric is moving in the right direction. Integration stays visible rather than dependent on memory.

One AI tool may need more than one integration record. A writing assistant used in proposal creation and again in client updates needs two records, different trigger, output, owner, review, and metric for each. Treating them as one integration produces blurred accountability and unreliable measurement.

Integration as part of approval

The checklist also becomes part of the Tool Approval Process from Chapter 8. Every new tool request gets the integration checklist completed alongside the approval documentation. A proposal that cannot answer all seven questions clearly is not ready for deployment. The right response is usually not rejection — it is resolving the design gap before the tool enters a live workflow. Better to spend a week on operational design than three months untangling inconsistent adoption afterward.

Managing Change When AI Replaces or Alters Human Tasks

Even with the checklist completed, integration involves change, and change always produces some friction, regardless of how well technology works. How that friction is handled determines whether the change sticks.

Three operational disciplines make the difference between an integration that survives the first quarter and one that does not:

1. Direct operational conversations before launch

Before the new integration goes live, have a conversation with every employee whose workflow will change. The conversation covers three things: what is changing operationally, why the integration is being introduced, and how the person's role will evolve afterward. The conversation also invites feedback, employees closest to the work often surface execution realities, edge cases, or workflow constraints that leadership did not see during the integration design (Dey et al., 2023). Integration maturity improves when workflow integration is treated as a collaborative operational design exercise rather than a top-down rollout.

2. A 30-day Operational Health Check™

Schedule a structured review for approximately thirty days after the integration goes live. Check three things:

- Is the integration functioning according to the checklist design, trigger firing, output flowing, handoff happening?
- Is the performance metric set in Question 7 moving in the intended direction?
- Are employees following the workflow structure consistently?

Early review is when small misalignments are still cheap to correct. Wait three months and the inconsistent behavior has embedded as habit, which is much harder to undo than fix.

3. Targeted fixes, not full redesigns

When something is not working, identify the specific operational breakdown rather than rebuilding the integration from scratch. Most integration failures trace to one of five points: an unclear trigger (Question 3), an ambiguous output handoff (Question 4), vague ownership (Question 5), an inconsistent review expectation (Question 6), or no measurement infrastructure (Question 7). Fixing the specific point is faster, cheaper, and less disruptive than starting over.

Integration discipline is the difference between a well-governed AI environment and a well-governed AI environment that delivers business results. The governance work in earlier chapters makes the environment manageable. The integration work in this chapter is what makes it productive.

Putting It into Practice

The implementation sequence for this chapter has four steps:

1. Map the three to five workflows that matter most. Document the workflows most critical to revenue, customer experience, operational efficiency, or scalability, in clear, step-by-step language. Each step gets a specific action, a defined input, and a measurable output. Pull in the people who perform the work; their view of bottlenecks and handoffs is more accurate than management's assumption.

2. Match the inventory to the workflows. Walk the AI inventory from Chapter 4 against the workflow maps. For each active system, identify the specific workflow step it belongs in. Systems that cannot be mapped to a specific step return to the Alignment Map from Chapter 9, operational availability without workflow placement rarely produces consistent value.

3. Run the Integration Checklist for every tool-workflow combination. All seven questions, fully answered, documented in an integration record. If any question cannot be answered clearly, pause deployment until the design gap is resolved. Premature deployment is the most common source of inconsistent adoption in this category.

4. Run the 30-day Operational Health Check™ for every new integration. Then add integration review to the quarterly governance cycle are systems still being used at the designated steps, are triggers still accurate, are review requirements still being followed, is the performance metric still moving in the intended direction? Integration is not a one-time event. It is a managed operational discipline.

When the four steps are complete, AI systems stop functioning as approved technologies operating adjacent to the business and start functioning as embedded operational infrastructure. Usage becomes consistent because the workflows themselves trigger it. Performance becomes measurable because execution patterns have been standardized. Improvement becomes possible because the data is clean enough to act on.

Figure 10.5 — Integrated AI Operating Workflow™

A Repeatable End-to-End Workflow That Embeds AI Into Operations

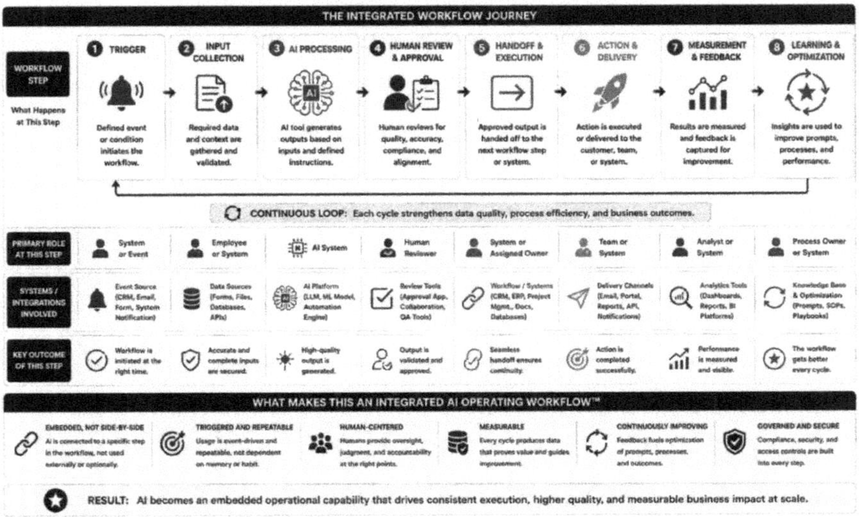

Integration is the final implementation layer that turns the broader framework from a governance concept into a functioning operating system. The next two chapters, the AI Decision-Making Model and the AI Operating System itself, are about making the whole thing self-sustaining.

Chapter 11: Building Your AI Decision-Making Model

A Framework for Every Future Choice

CHAPTER OUTCOMES

At the end of this chapter, you will be able to:

- **Identify** why AI tools fail at the integration level despite strong technology.
- **Use the AI Integration Checklist™** to embed AI into recurring operational workflows.
- **Design workflow triggers,** ownership, review controls, and measurable outputs for AI systems.
- **Standardize AI usage** across departments to improve consistency and operational performance.
- **Conduct 30-day Operational Health Check™** reviews to validate adoption and workflow execution.
- **Transform AI systems** from optional tools into embedded operational infrastructure.

Why Ad Hoc AI Decisions Are Costing You More Than You Realize

Every AI tool inside the business exists because someone decided. An employee saw a demo. The department head got frustrated with a slow process. A consultant recommended a platform. A competitor mentioned it at a conference. The individual decisions usually look reasonable in isolation. The problem is what happens when dozens of those decisions are made independently — without a shared framework guiding them.

Over time, the inventory accumulates. Tools overlap. Costs grow across departments. Risk expands through systems evaluated by inconsistent standards. Leadership loses visibility into why certain platforms were approved, who approved them, and whether they are producing measurable business value.

The size of the gap is meaningful. Research on AI adoption maturity has consistently found that companies without strategic integration and structured governance experience initiative failure rates near 88%, while companies operating under coordinated management models reach success rates as high as 74% (Westover, 2025). The difference is not the stack of technology. It is whether adoption happens through disciplined management or through reactive, fragmented decisions.

The pattern shows up across companies of every size. Consider a professional services firm running on $3.8 million in revenue. Over two years, leadership has approved three significant AI platforms, a workflow automation system signed off by operations after a vendor demo, an AI content generation platform adopted by marketing after an industry conference, and an AI analytics platform approved by the owner after a consulting recommendation. None of the decisions looked unreasonable at the time. When leadership eventually reviews the broader AI environment, the firm finds overlapping capability between two of the three platforms, inconsistent approval standards across the three decisions, unclear ownership for two of them, and no documented connection from any of the three to a measurable business outcome. Spending up. Operational complexity is up. Governance exposure is up. Strategic value is unclear.

FIGURE 11.1
Ad Hoc AI vs Structured AI Decision-Making™

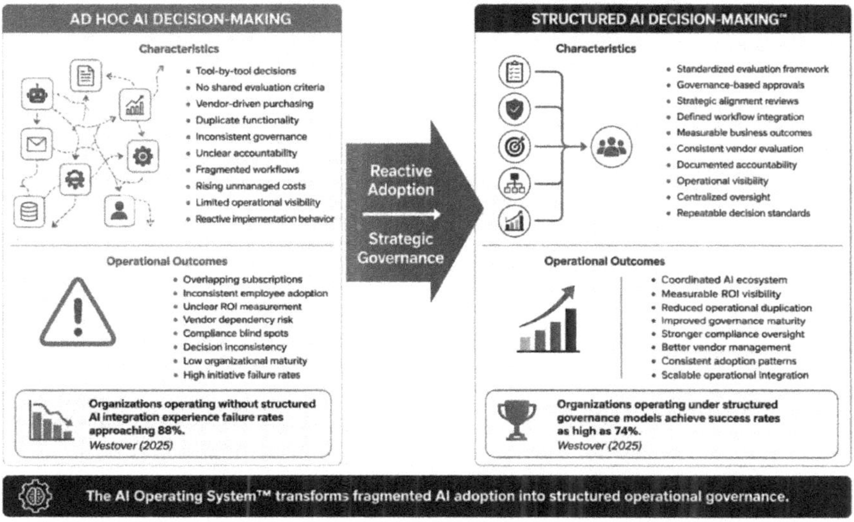

The fix is not slower adoption. The fix is a structured decision-making model, one repeatable framework that evaluates every AI proposal consistently against the same set of business, operational, governance, financial, and risk standards. When the framework exists, business stops debating each tool from scratch. Vendor enthusiasm, urgency, and isolated departmental pressure stop driving outcomes. Every proposal, regardless of who is making it, gets weighed against the same standards.

Everything in this book up to this point has produced the inputs the framework needs: an inventory, a cost map, performance measurements, governance controls, a risk assessment, and an alignment view. What remains is combining those inputs into a decision-making rhythm that governs every future AI choice the company makes.

The AI Adoption Decision Framework™

Five questions. Every new AI proposal clears all five before approval. The framework does not slow adoption; it makes adoption defensible.

FIGURE 11.2

The AI Adoption Decision Framework™

A Structured Five-Question Model for Evaluating Every Future AI Decision

Applied consistently, the framework produces a different operational outcome. New tools enter the business because they satisfy a defined set of standards, not because they were persuasive in a demo or urgent in the moment. Approval becomes documented, repeatable, and defensible. Vendor relationships operate under clearer accountability. Inventory growth slows naturally — not because innovation is being suppressed, but because the bar is real.

How to Evaluate AI Vendors Like a Business Owner, not a Consumer

AI vendors are skilled at making adoption feel low risk: free trials, low introductory pricing, polished demos, customer testimonials. The tactics work because the decision looks cheap and reversible. But a business is not making a personal productivity purchase. It is entering a vendor relationship that affects business continuity, data governance, workflow execution, and long-term operational dependency.

Companies that evaluate vendors using consumer criteria, features, usability, the impressive demo — discover the structural issues only after dependency has formed. By that point, exiting is expensive. Six evaluation areas separate consumer-style adoption from operator-grade adoption:

FIGURE 11.3

AI Vendor Evaluation Matrix™

A Structured Governance Model for Evaluating AI Vendors Before Approval

VENDOR GOVERNANCE REVIEW FRAMEWORK™

EVALUATION CATEGORY	KEY GOVERNANCE QUESTIONS	OPERATIONAL RISK IF IGNORED
1 VENDOR STABILITY	• How long has the vendor operated? • Is the company financially stable? • Does the vendor support organizations of similar size? • Are credible client references available?	• Vendor collapse risk • Service instability • Unsupported implementation environments • Operational disruption
2 DATA SOVEREIGNTY & PRIVACY	• Does the vendor use customer data for model training? • Where is data stored? • What retention policies exist? • Is third-party sharing permitted? • Are privacy protections documented?	• Regulatory exposure • Confidential data leakage • Compliance violations • Loss of governance control
3 OPERATIONAL COMPATIBILITY	• Does the system integrate into current workflows? • Will it duplicate existing functionality? • Is implementation complexity manageable? • Can employees realistically adopt the system?	• Workflow fragmentation • Employee adoption failure • Redundant technology costs • Operational inefficiency
4 FINANCIAL SUSTAINABILITY	• What are the full long-term costs? • Are pricing increases predictable? • Are usage-based fees scalable? • What internal labor costs exist?	• Budget instability • Hidden operational costs • Subscription sprawl • Long-term financial inefficiency
5 GOVERNANCE & ACCOUNTABILITY	• Are review requirements documented? • Are approval structures defined? • Does the vendor support auditability? • Can leadership maintain oversight visibility?	• Weak governance enforcement • Decision accountability gaps • Reduced operational visibility • Inconsistent compliance controls
6 VENDOR DEPENDENCY RISK	• Could the organization transition vendors within 30 days? • Is contingency planning documented? • Are export and migration options available? • Would disruption materially affect operations?	• Vendor lock-in • Operational disruption • Loss of continuity • Strategic dependency exposure

HIGH-MATURITY ORGANIZATIONS EVALUATE VENDORS BEFORE ADOPTION

Better operational alignment	Stronger data protection	Reduced implementation failure	Improved vendor accountability	Lower long-term operational risk

Structured vendor evaluation transforms AI purchasing from reactive procurement into operational governance.

1. Contract structure and renewal terms

Contract length. Automatic renewal provisions. Cancellation deadlines. Pricing-adjustment clauses. Many AI vendors default to annual contracts that renew automatically unless cancellation happens inside a narrow notification window, usually 30 to 90 days before renewal. Companies discover these provisions only after renewal has fired. Map renewal dates, escalation language, and cancellation procedures into the inventory before dependency forms.

2. Data ownership and portability

Confirm in writing that all operational data submitted to the platform remains owned by the business. Review terms for any language granting broad rights around data usage, retention, model training, aggregation, or third-party sharing. Just as important: confirm whether data can be exported in a usable format if the company terminates the relationship. Vendor lock-in frequently occurs not because cancellation is impossible but because retrieval is operationally disruptive or financially expensive.

3. Support accountability and escalation

Once integrated, AI systems supporting important workflows become business continuity dependencies. What level of support is included? What is the response-time commitments by issue severity? What is the escalation path when an operational problem occurs? Sales-cycle support claims and actual operating support are often different in degree. Understanding the difference before the platform is embedded in critical workflows, not after.

4. Vendor stability and long-term viability

The AI vendor landscape is moving fast and not every platform operating today will survive. Before building core workflows around a system, ask: how long has the company existed, is the revenue model stable, does the product roadmap suggest continued investment? You do not need to financially audit every vendor. You do need enough information to judge whether the provider is likely to remain a stable partner over the next several years.

5. References from comparable businesses

Vendors highlight enterprise case studies that often do not translate to smaller companies with tighter budgets and lighter technical resources. Ask for references from organizations close to your size, industry, and operating structure (Sánchez et al., 2025). Those conversations consistently surface implementation realities, onboarding pain, workflow constraints, support quality, feature limitations that sales demos do not.

6. Exit conditions

Understand operational disengagement before commitment. Termination penalties. Data deletion procedures. Integration shutdown requirements. Workflow migration complexity. Some vendors make disengagement straightforward; others build friction that keeps customers subscribed past the point where the relationship still delivers value. Knowing the exit conditions in advance is not pessimism. It is responsible for operational planning.

Applied consistently, these six standards shift the nature of the vendor conversation. Leadership stops behaving like a consumer evaluating a product and starts behaving like an operator evaluating a partnership. Vendors respond differently when the buyer is asking governance questions, requesting accountability, and demonstrating procurement discipline. That alone improves negotiation quality and long-term decision-making.

Creating a Standing AI Adoption Policy

The Decision Framework and vendor standards only deliver consistency if they are documented. Without a written policy, the framework gets applied unevenly. Tools proposed by senior employees get less scrutiny than tools proposed by junior staff. Recommendations from trusted advisors move faster than standard vendor outreach. Decisions made during busy periods bypass the evaluation that would happen under less pressure. The inconsistencies are rarely intentional. They are predictable.

The Standing AI Adoption Policy™ closes that gap. Two pages, five sections. The objective is clarity, not compliance theater.

Section 1 — Scope. The policy applies to (employees, contractors, consultants, third-party vendors) and what decisions fall inside its boundaries (new tool adoption, upgrades to existing platforms, expanded workflow usage, changes involving new data categories).

Section 2 — The Five-Question Evaluation Framework. All five questions stated explicitly. Reference the evaluation form, where it lives, and who reviews it. This is what converts the framework from concept into required procedure.

Section 3 — Approval Authority. Named approver. Most small and mid-sized companies are best served by centralizing authority under the owner or a designated operational leader. No system goes into business use without approval through the documented process. When unauthorized tools are discovered, the response is retroactive evaluation — usage paused until approval is granted or denied, but not punitive. Punitive responses suppress disclosure (back to Chapter 2).

Section 4 — Review Cadence. Monthly operational reviews. Quarterly governance audits. Annual reassessment. Trigger-based review for systems failing benchmarks or exceeding budget thresholds. Governance is an active discipline, not a one-time approval.

Section 5 — Controlled Exception Process. How expedited approvals are requested. Who can grant provisional approval. How long it stays provisional before full evaluation is required. Cap on how many exceptions can run simultaneously, so the exception path does not become the default path.

Distribute the policy through the same channels that introduced the governance documents from Chapter 8. Short rollout meeting. Written summary within 24 hours. Add to onboarding for new hires and contractors. The policy that is easy to find gets followed; the policy that takes effort to locate gets bypassed.

Retroactive evaluation

After the policy is live, run the same five-question framework against every active AI system already in the inventory. Treat each existing tool as if it were being proposed for the first time under the new standard (Sadiq et al., 2021). Some systems will pass easily. Others will reveal gaps, weak cost justification, governance readiness never considered, no measurable outcome ever defined. Tools that would not be approved today should be flagged for the next renewal review.

Retroactive evaluation is among the most valuable governance exercises the business can run, because it surfaces the patterns in past adoption practice. Weak cost discipline. Governance considered it too late. Strategic alignment is never tested. Those patterns tell leadership where future governance attention needs to live.

FIGURE 11.4

The AI Maturity Progression Model™

How Organizations Evolve from Reactive AI Adoption to Structured AI Governance

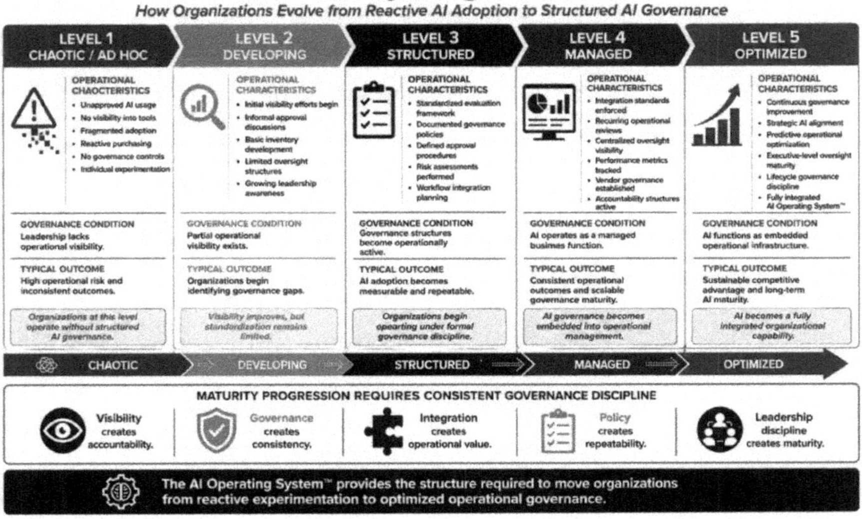

Putting It into Practice Three implementation priorities:

1. Formalize the Decision Framework as a one-page document. All five questions in full, plus references to the Integration Checklist (Chapter 10) and the vendor evaluation standards above. Store with the governance documents. This becomes the master evaluation tool for every future AI adoption decision.

2. Run the retroactive audit on every active AI system. Apply all five framework questions to each tool. Document results in inventory. Systems failing Question 1 or 2 (no real problem, no value justification) go to the next cancellation review. Systems failing Question 3 (data risk) move immediately into the remediation process from Chapter 7. Systems failing Questions 4 or 5 (fit, governance plan) get a documented improvement plan with a named owner, a defined objective, and a specific deadline.

FIGURE 11.5
The AI Decision Implementation Framework™
Turning AI Decisions into Measurable Operational Outcomes

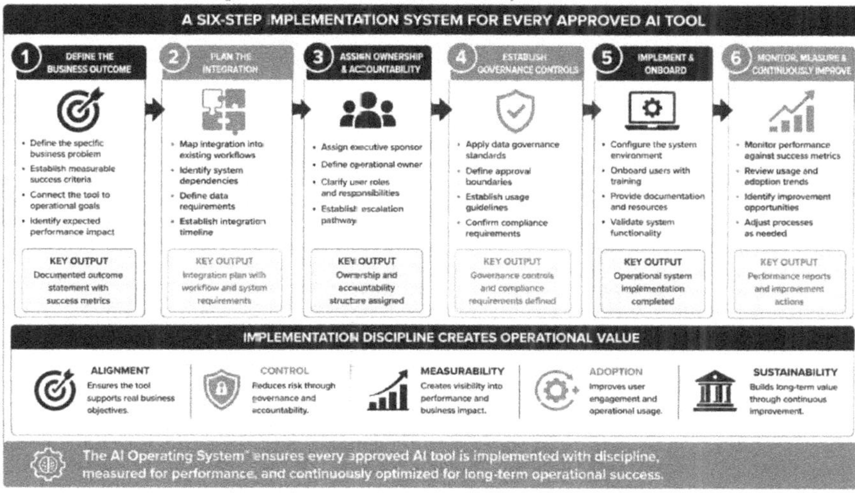

3. Stand up the Standing AI Adoption Policy. Five sections. Two pages. Reviewed for clarity by at least one additional team member before finalization. Introduced in a short operational meeting, reinforced by a written summary, embedded in onboarding. Add a recurring policy-verification check to the quarterly governance review, were new adoptions in the prior quarter routed through the framework, or did any bypass it?

When the three priorities are in place, every future AI decision operates against the same standards. New tools enter because they satisfy defined business, governance, finance, and operational test, not because a demo was persuasive or a competitor mentioned the platform at a conference. Vendor relationships operate under clearer accountability. Inventory growth becomes deliberate. Governance and strategy stay aligned.

That consistency is the long-term outcome. The framework is not designed only to improve visibility into current AI usage. It is designed to discipline every future decision the company makes about AI, with the same accountability and consistency the rest of the operating system requires.

Chapter 12: The AI Operating System™

Running AI as a Permanent Business Function

CHAPTER OUTCOMES

At the end of this chapter, you will be able to:

Operate AI governance on a recurring monthly, quarterly, and annual cadence
using The AI Operating Calendar™ to maintain continuous visibility and control.

Keep the AI Operating System™ current and accurate
by maintaining inventory, spending, performance, alignment, and risk information on an ongoing basis.

Recalculate value and performance regularly
by updating scorecards, ROI, and alignment to ensure AI investments continue to deliver business impact.

Sustain strong governance and mitigate risk
by enforcing policies, monitoring triggers, reviewing vendor risk, and addressing governance gaps before they escalate.

Align AI with business strategy
by continuously mapping tools to business objectives and removing systems that no longer support strategic goals.

Institutionalize AI as a permanent business function
by embedding roles, accountability, and review rhythms that turn AI governance into a disciplined, repeatable operating system.

Eleven chapters back, the framework began with a simple diagnosis: AI was already inside the business, and no one had written the rules for how it operates. Visibility was the starting point. Governance, alignment, and integration came next. Each chapter built one component of the management infrastructure AI deserves and most companies have never installed around it.

What sits in front of the business now is the system.

A documented inventory. A real cost picture. Performance scorecards. A risk classification. A written governance policy. An alignment map. An integration discipline. A decision framework for everything that comes next. Each component is useful on its own. The compounding value comes from running them together — every month, every quarter, every year — as a single managed function.

This chapter is about that running. None of the previous chapters produces lasting value if its outputs are completed once and then filed. An inventory that stops being updated becomes inaccurate within months. A cost baseline that is not reviewed allows spending to drift upward without accountability. Governance policies that are not reinforced lose operational relevance. Performance measurements that are not recalculated stop reflecting current business outcomes. Every component of The AI Operating System™ was designed to operate as an ongoing management discipline rather than a completed implementation exercise.

The companies receiving the strongest returns from AI governance are not the ones that completed an audit once (Westover, 2025). They are the ones that turned AI oversight into a permanent business function — supported by a recurring cadence, structured review cycles, and continuous visibility — and held that discipline through quarters when easier priorities were competing for attention.

This chapter shows what that looks like in operation.

FIGURE 12.1 **The AI Governance Ecosystem Alignment Map™**

The five interconnected domains of the AI Governance Ecosystem and the outcomes they deliver.

Governance Domain	Primary Purpose	Key Components	Current Strength	Strategic Outcome	Alignment Status
1 PEOPLE & CULTURE Build the right foundation for responsible AI use.	Align people, roles, behaviors, and capabilities with responsible AI use and accountability.	• Clear roles & responsibilities • AI literacy & training • Ethical culture & accountability • Change management & adoption	↑ Strong High training completion and role clarity.	Engaged, skilled teams that use AI responsibly and effectively.	ALIGNED ✓
2 POLICIES & GOVERNANCE Establish the rules and guardrails that govern AI.	Define policies, standards, and processes that ensure safe, legal, and compliant AI operations.	• AI usage policies • Data privacy & security • Risk management • Compliance & regulatory alignment • Approval & review processes	↑ Strong Policies are mature and consistently enforced.	Governed AI operations with low risk and high compliance.	ALIGNED ✓
3 PROCESSES & WORKFLOWS Embed AI into business processes with structure and consistency.	Integrate AI into workflows with standardization, oversight, and continuous improvement.	• Standardized evaluation • Implementation & integration • Human oversight & review • Monitoring & continuous improvement	→ Moderate Processes exist but lack full standardization.	Efficient, reliable processes that deliver consistent AI outcomes.	PARTIAL (!)
4 TECHNOLOGY & DATA Use secure, scalable tools and quality data to power AI.	Ensure the right technology, data, and architecture support trustworthy AI performance.	• Tool inventory & management • Secure data handling • Model & output quality • Technology architecture • Vendor & third-party management	↑ Strong Technology and data foundation are robust.	Secure, scalable systems that produce reliable, accurate AI outputs.	ALIGNED ✓
5 MEASUREMENT & VALUE Measure performance, manage risk, and demonstrate value from AI.	Track outcomes, manage risk, and prove business value through measurable evidence.	• KPIs & performance scorecards • ROI & cost management • Risk & compliance monitoring • Reporting & stakeholder communication	↑ Strong Clear metrics and reporting drive visibility and accountability.	Measurable business value and continuous improvement.	ALIGNED ✓

ALIGNMENT STATUS KEY

- ✓ ALIGNED — Domain is effectively managed and delivering measurable outcomes.
- (!) PARTIAL — Domain is in progress but needs further improvement.
- ⊗ UNALIGNED — Domain is not aligned and requires immediate attention.

RECOMMENDED ACTION

- Maintain momentum and continue strengthening this domain.
- Implement improvement plan and increase focus in this domain.
- Address root causes and realign to achieve desired outcomes.

STRATEGIC PURPOSE

The AI Governance Ecosystem works as five interconnected domains. When each domain is aligned and working together, organizations achieve lower risk, higher performance, and sustainable AI value.

This map helps leadership see where the system is strong, where to focus next, and how to drive continuous governance maturity.

Why the Audit Is the Beginning, Not the End

Most business improvement initiatives follow a project pattern: diagnose, implement, complete, move on. Defined start, defined end. AI does not work that way. AI is an ongoing function — tools change, vendors change, workflows change, employee usage changes, regulatory ground shifts. A framework that resets the view of all of that once a year, refreshes it once a quarter, and monitors it once a month is the management equivalent of running monthly financials. A framework that does the same review once and considers the job done produces the opposite of governance.

Compare AI governance to financial management. Companies do not audit their books once, fix a few items, and stop reviewing financials. They reconcile monthly. They run quarterly cash-flow reviews. They close the year and reset for the next one. The ongoing discipline is what produces visibility into how the business is actually performing, and it is what allows leadership to act before problems compound.

AI deserves the same treatment for the same reasons. The Audit in this book established the organization's first complete operational baseline — what exists, what it costs, what it produces, what it risks, where governance is missing. The baseline is real. The baseline is also dated the day it is captured. AI adoption keeps moving. Vendor terms keep changing. New tools keep entering the business. Workflows keep evolving. Without a recurring cadence, the baseline degrades quietly, and within nine to twelve months the organization is back in the pre-audit condition — without having ever consciously decided to be (Sadiq et al., 2021).

The audit is not the conclusion of governance. It is the foundation. Running it once produces visibility. Running it on a rhythm produces capability.

The AI Operating Calendar™ — Monthly, Quarterly, and Annual Rhythms

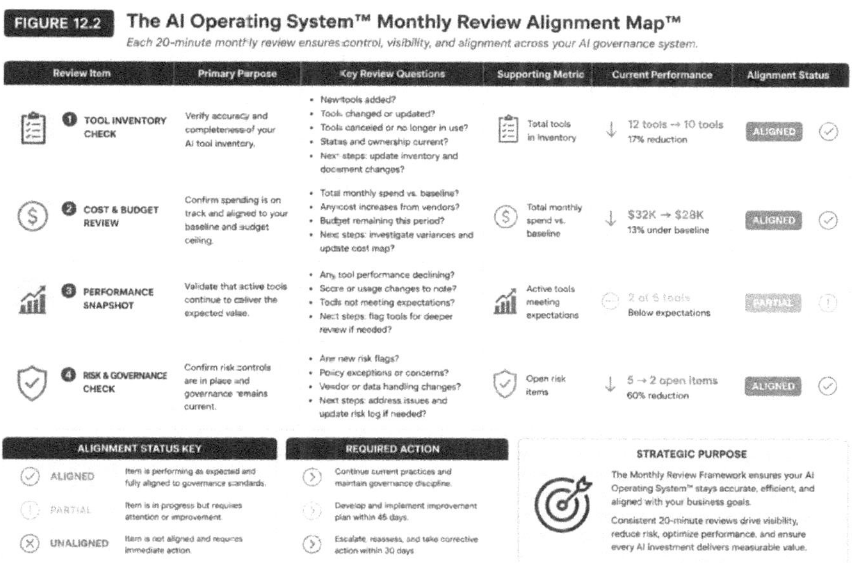

FIGURE 12.2 The AI Operating System™ Monthly Review Alignment Map™

Each 20-minute monthly review ensures control, visibility, and alignment across your AI governance system.

The Operating Calendar is three recurring layers — each with a different cadence, a different time commitment, and a different purpose. Running together, they make AI governance operational rather than aspirational.

Monthly review (15–20 minutes)

FIGURE 12.3 The AI Operating System™ Escalation & Trigger Response Alignment Map™

Detect Early. Respond Quickly. Protect Value. Prevent Risk.

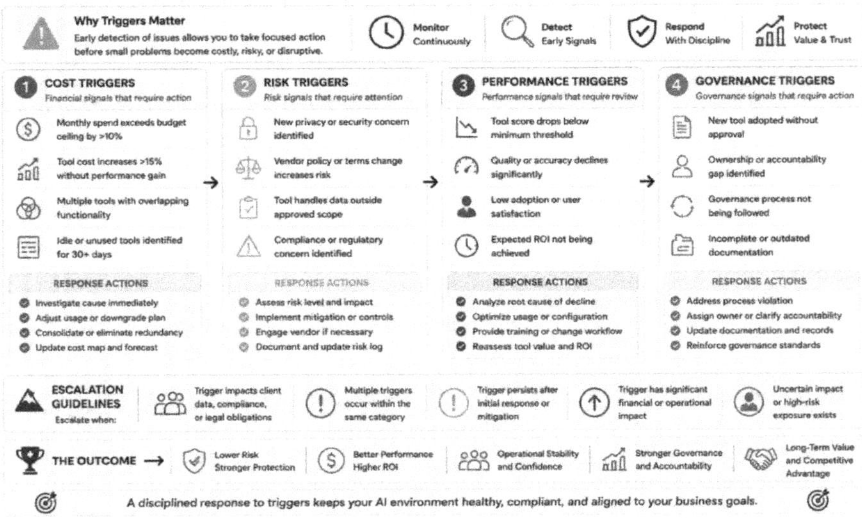

Same day each month. Treated as a fixed operational commitment, not a flexible task. Consistency matters more than duration — the objective is continuous visibility, not periodic cleanup. Four questions:

Inventory. Have any new AI tools, embedded features, browser extensions, or integrations entered the environment since last month?

Spending. Are vendor costs, usage-based pricing, or renewals tracking against the baseline?

Trigger conditions. Any vendor policy changes, declining performance scores, upcoming contract renewals, or governance exceptions to act on? Each one gets a named owner, a next step, and a deadline before the meeting ends.

Governance friction. Did any policies prove hard to follow this month? Did any workflows develop outside the approval process? Surface and fix; do not redesign.

Quarterly governance review (~45 minutes)

The primary management session. Most companies will get the most from running this alongside the quarterly business or financial review, so AI stays integrated with broader operations rather than isolated as a technology discussion. Six activities:

- Update the AI Performance Scorecard™ for every active tool.
- Recalculate ROI for the highest-cost or most operationally critical systems.
- Refresh the Alignment Map™ — does every active system still support a current strategic objective?
- Reassess risk for any system with material changes in vendor terms, workflow usage, or data handling.
- Review governance documents for operational relevance and update what no longer matches reality.
- Re-evaluating dependency tiers — has anything become more critical or less strategically relevant since last quarter?

Annual review (several hours)

The deepest cycle — and ideally aligned to annual strategic planning so AI direction stays tied to broader business priorities. Functions as a refreshed Audit, but faster than the original because the framework already exists. The annual cycle covers all quarterly activities plus three strategic resets:

New operational cost baseline. Reflects current spending and organizational scale, not assumptions twelve months old.

Strategic alignment review. Does the AI portfolio support the direction the business intends to pursue over the next year, or the direction the business was pursuing previously?

Full shadow-AI reassessment. What new employee-adopted tools, embedded vendor capabilities, or unofficial integrations have entered the environment over the past year? Even strong governance cultures accumulate some — the annual cycle is when to surface them (Hansen et al., 2024).

Over time, the recurring rhythm itself becomes the most valuable asset the framework produces. Each cycle strengthens operational intelligence. Inventories get more accurate. Performance measurements get more reliable. Risk assessments get more informed. Decisions get faster, because the standards have already been settled and the data has already been gathered. Governance maturity does not happen at a moment. It compounds.

Scaling the System as Your Business Grows

The Operating System was designed to fit the business as it is today. Growth changes the math. A governance structure that works for a ten-person company with eight AI tools will need refinement when that company becomes a forty-person operation with thirty tools across four departments. The principles do not change. The structure supporting them has to scale alongside the business.

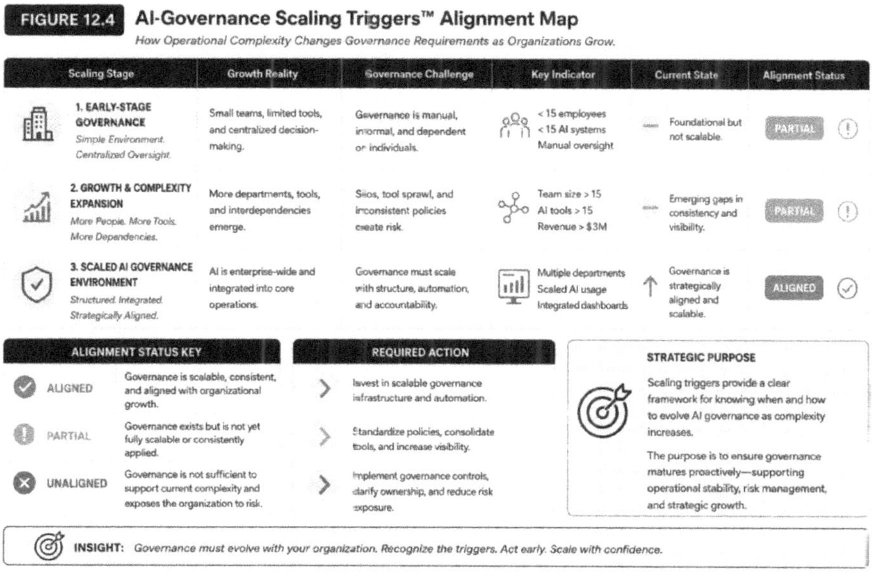

Three scaling triggers tend to drive the structural updates:

Trigger 1 — Team size (~15+ employees)

Single-approver governance starts producing friction. One individual cannot evaluate every tool proposal, maintain review cycles, and oversee governance responsibilities across a larger operating environment. Distribute approval authority: department or operational managers approve lower-risk tools within predefined budget and governance thresholds; executive leadership retains oversight for higher-risk systems, larger spending, or strategically significant integrations. The framework stays standardized; the approval responsibility distributes.

Trigger 2 — Tool count (~15+ active systems)

Detailed inventory review during the monthly cycle becomes impractical. Add a simplified operational dashboard summarizing the environment at a glance This chapter shows what that looks like in operation: total monthly AI spend, active tool count by category, systems with trigger flags, vendor renewals approaching in the next sixty days, elevated governance issues requiring executive attention. The dashboard supplements the detailed inventory rather than replacing it.

Trigger 3 — Revenue growth (~$3M+ in annual revenue)

AI spending often becomes large enough to deserve formal integration into financial planning — a dedicated AI operating budget, formal spending allocations by category, escalation procedures for spend above thresholds, AI investment discussions inside annual strategic planning (Badghish & Soomro, 2024). Treating AI spend like a budget category instead of a collection of vendor invoices is what allows the company to plan it deliberately.

Two scaling disciplines apply across all three triggers:

Secondary inventory ownership. Assign a designated operations or administrative owner to maintain the inventory between formal reviews — document new tools, vendor changes, cancellations, and operational adjustments as they happen. Executive oversight stays. Daily maintenance distributes.

Proactive governance adaptation. When the business enters a new industry, customer segment, or operational function that carries different regulatory obligations or data-handling expectations, update the governance documentation before the operational expansion, not after. Retrofitting governance under duress is always more expensive than building it ahead.

Communicating Your AI Strategy to Your Team, Clients, and Stakeholders

A working AI governance system creates value in two directions at once. Internally, it gives the organization visibility, accountability, and structured oversight. Externally, it communicates to clients, partners, vendors, and investors that the company runs AI deliberately rather than reactively. That external signal is increasingly meaningful, yet most businesses have not formally considered AI governance as part of their broader positioning.

Different audiences need different framings of the same underlying discipline.

FIGURE 12.5 AI-Governance Trust & Communication Framework™ Alignment Map

How Structured AI Governance Builds Confidence Across Employees, Clients, and Stakeholders

Internally — operational reinforcement

Three practical disciplines:

Reference the framework during routine decisions. When a new tool gets proposed, reference the Decision Framework. When AI costs come up in budget discussions, reference the baseline. When AI-assisted outputs get produced, reference the review requirements. Routine reference is what turns policy into habit.

Share brief governance review summaries. After monthly and quarterly reviews, send a short update to the team — what was reviewed, what changed, what is being adjusted. Reinforces that governance is an active function, not paperwork.

Keep the documents genuinely accessible. Linked in team communication channels, onboarding materials, workflow references. Policies stored deep inside disconnected folders do not influence real decisions because no one consults them.

Externally — client and stakeholder communication

Clients generally are not interested in the mechanics of governance frameworks. They are interested in whether the business handles their data, workflows, and deliverables responsibly. Develop a concise plain-language statement covering three points: the business uses AI to improve efficiency and service quality; all systems go through formal evaluation and approval before operational use; documented policies govern how client information interacts with AI systems. Include this proactively where it matters — onboarding materials, proposals, service agreements, client trust documentation. The communication is most valuable in professional services, healthcare, financial services, legal, and other industries where operational trust is part of the buying decision (Pumplun et al., 2019).

Stakeholder and investor communication need more specificity. Vague claims about "responsible AI usage" no longer signal maturity. Describe the framework concretely — a centralized inventory, defined cost baselines, recurring performance scorecards, documented governance policies, operational risk assessments, alignment reviews, and a recurring governance cycle. Specificity reads as maturity. It also directly addresses one of the largest concerns holding back broader enterprise trust in AI right now, 77% of organizations identify governance uncertainty and operational immaturity as barriers to adoption (Poon et al., 2025).

Vendor negotiations — a side benefit

Companies operating inside a structured governance framework negotiate from a different position. Spend levels, operational dependencies, performance expectations, and contingency options are all documented before vendor discussions begin. When pricing changes, the company has performance data and baselines to respond with. When terms conflict with governance requirements, the conflict can be named specifically. When vendors propose expanded services, the proposal goes through the same Decision Framework as anything else. Operational discipline produces informational leverage, and informational leverage produces better vendor outcomes.

Turning AI Control into a Competitive Advantage

Most companies are still operating AI fragmentedly. Tools adopted without governance. Costs accumulated without accountability. Risks expanding without visibility. Decisions made without a consistent evaluation framework. That is the operational baseline across much of the market right now. Most businesses do not fix it until problems, financial waste, regulatory pressure, or an incident forces governance attention reactively rather than strategically.

Figure 12.6 – Turning AI Control into a Competitive Advantage™

Structured Governance Today. Stronger Decisions Tomorrow. Lasting Business Impact.

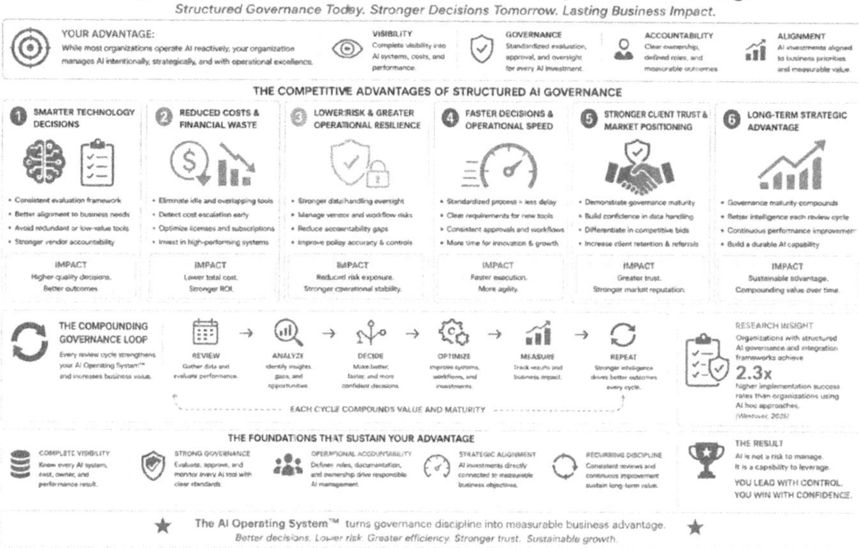

By completing The AI Operating System™, the business has already moved past that baseline. The advantage created is not decorative. It compounds in four directions over time:

Financial. Lower spending on idle or overlapping tools, faster identification of cost escalation, capital concentrated on systems producing measurable returns. The savings recur, because the framework keeps spending aligned to priorities rather than allowing the inventory to grow unchecked. Cumulative multi-year impact frequently exceeds the value of any single tool in the stack (Westover, 2025).

Operational risk. Each recurring risk assessment strengthens visibility into data handling, vendor dependencies, and accountability gaps. Each documented accountability framework reduces the likelihood of unmanaged decisions touching sensitive outcomes (Pumplun et al., 2019).

Speed. Structured evaluation accelerates decisions rather than slowing them. Employees know what to bring. Leadership knows how it will be evaluated. Standards are settled in advance. Removing ambiguity removes friction.

Market positioning. Clients increasingly evaluate vendors on governance maturity, not just technology adoption. Companies able to describe documented oversight, data protections, and recurring review cycles win regulated-industry and enterprise work that competitors cannot credibly compete for.

The long-term winners in this category will not be the companies adopting the most tools fastest. They will be the companies that developed the discipline to govern AI consistently, evaluate investments intelligently, integrate systems strategically, and maintain visibility as adoption keeps evolving. That governance infrastructure is a competitive capability — and one that scales ahead of competitors still struggling with fragmentation and reactive decisions.

Putting It into Motion

The framework is built. What remains is running it.

Immediate actions to activate the operating rhythm:

Schedule the monthly review as a recurring commitment. Same day each month. Twenty minutes. Calendar invite includes direct links to the inventory, cost baseline, and governance dashboard. Agenda includes the four monthly questions. The recurrence matters more than the elegance — never miss the monthly review, regardless of how busy the month becomes.

Schedule the quarterly governance review. Same week each quarter. Forty-five minutes. Calendar invite includes links to the Scorecard, Alignment

Map, governance policies, risk assessments, and vendor documentation. Agenda includes the six quarterly activities. Running this alongside the quarterly business review is usually the right call.

Schedule the annual review. Block several hours during the same week each year — ideally aligned to annual strategic planning. The annual review resets baselines, refreshes strategic alignment, and benchmarks governance maturity. Scheduling it now, even months in advance, is what keeps it from getting deferred when other priorities compete.

Assign secondary inventory ownership. Distribute operational maintenance across the business. The designated owner documents new tools, vendor changes, pricing adjustments, cancellations, and workflow modifications as they happen, not as a monthly catch-up.

Develop the external governance statement. Plain language. Three points (tools used to improve efficiency, formal evaluation before adoption, documented data-handling policies). Add onboarding materials, service agreements, proposal documentation, and client trust documentation where appropriate.

Make governance permanent inside leadership rhythm. Add a standing AI governance update to recurring leadership meetings. Even a one-minute confirmation, monthly activities completed, spending aligned, no elevated trigger conditions, reinforces that AI is now a managed function rather than a temporary initiative.

The companies that produce the strongest long-term outcomes from AI will not be the ones adopting the most tools fastest. They will be the ones running the discipline above, month after month, quarter after quarter, year after year, until governance becomes the way the business operates rather than a project the business completed.

The Operating System was designed to produce exactly that. Not a one-time cleanup. Not a temporary initiative. A permanent management capability that lets the business run AI with visibility, accountability, and strategic control as the environment keeps moving.

The system is built. Now run it.

Conclusion: What You've Actually Built

And Why It Matters More Than You Think

Imagine two versions of the same business, twelve months from now.

In the first, AI adoption has continued the way it was running before this framework arrived. The inventory has grown by another dozen tools that nobody fully tracked. Spending has expanded quietly across credit cards and departmental budgets. Two vendors have made unilateral pricing changes; one of them was missed until renewal. A client raised a concern about an AI-generated output that should never have gone out without review. Leadership still cannot answer, in a sentence, what AI is costing the company in total or what it is producing in return. The business has more AI than it had a year ago. It has no more visibility.

In the second version, the company has been running the system.

The inventory is current. The cost picture is documented. Every active tool has a named owner, a defined business outcome, a tracked performance score, and a risk classification. Three underperforming systems were retired during the quarterly review. Two strategically aligned tools got expanded because the performance data supported it. A new vendor change triggered the review process before anything was approved. Leadership can answer, in a sentence each, what the AI environment costs, what it produces, what it risks, and where it is going next. The business has more AI than it had a year ago. It also has the operational capability to keep running AI deliberately as adoption continues.

The technology is the same in both versions. The companies are the same size. The difference is one year of operational discipline.

That difference is what this book is about.

What You Built

Each chapter installed one piece of the operating infrastructure:

Visibility — a complete, current inventory of every AI system operating across the business (Chapters 2–4).

Financial discipline — a real cost picture across direct, variable, integration, and labor costs, with a defended baseline (Chapter 5).

Performance measurement — the AI Performance Scorecard™ and the AI ROI Evaluation Framework™ tied to measurable business outcomes (Chapter 6).

Risk management — four risk categories, a ten-question assessment, the AI Decision Accountability Framework™, and vendor contingency planning (Chapter 7).

Governance — three documents (Usage Policy, Tool Approval Process, Data Access Protocol) and the discipline to keep them current (Chapter 8).

Strategic alignment — the AI-to-Outcome Alignment Map™ and the Strategic Prioritization Framework (Chapter 9).

Operational integration — the AI Integration Checklist™ and the 30-day Operational Health Check™ (Chapter 10).

Decision-making — the AI Adoption Decision Framework™ and the Standing AI Adoption Policy™ (Chapter 11).

Operating rhythm — the AI Operating Calendar™ with monthly, quarterly, and annual cycles (Chapter 12).

These are not nine separate improvements. They are nine layers of a single operational management system. Each layer makes the next one possible. The inventory makes cost mapping reliable. The cost map makes performance measurement honest. The performance data makes governance decisions defensible. The governance structure makes the operating calendar credible. The calendar makes every part of the system durable.

Most organizations operating AI today have none of these layers consistently. A few have one or two. Almost none have all nine running together. The gap between organizations managing AI systematically and organizations operating reactively is real, and over time it compounds. Each governance cycle strengthens decision quality. Each recurring review improves visibility. Each cost evaluation tightens financial discipline. The advantage is not produced once. It is produced every cycle, in perpetuity, as long as the system keeps running.

The Action Is the Advantage

The hardest part is over. The framework exists. The standards are written. The cadence is defined. What separates the businesses that capture the advantage from the businesses that fade back to the pre-audit condition is not insight or capability. It is execution.

This is the point where most operational improvement initiatives lose momentum. The concepts are understood. The gaps are visible. The plan looks clear on paper. Then normal business pressures return. Quarterly priorities compete for attention. The urgency around implementation softens. The monthly review gets postponed once, then twice, then quietly drops off the calendar. Within a year, the framework that produced the original audit is documentation rather than discipline.

The fix is not heroic. The fix is mechanical.

The companies that get the most out of this framework are not the ones that understand it most deeply. They are the ones that operationalized it first and held the rhythm through the quarters when easier priorities were competing. The first monthly review is what creates accountability. The first quarterly governance cycle is what produces real measurable baselines. The first annual reset is when the framework starts to compound. From there, every cycle is faster than the last, because leadership is refining an active system rather than building from scratch.

Three operational characteristics develop inside companies that stay disciplined:

Decisions become faster. Standards are settled. Data is current. Leadership stops relitigating every tool decision and starts making them inside a known framework.

Confidence becomes visible. Vendor negotiations, budget conversations, client communications, and strategic planning all reflect the underlying governance maturity. The signal reaches the people the business needs to reach.

Risk becomes manageable. Not zero — never zero. But surfaced, classified, owned, and reviewed on a schedule. The exposure shifts from "undefined background concern" to "documented operational discipline."

Those three characteristics compound. Better decisions, repeated consistently, produce stronger outcomes. Stronger outcomes strengthen the framework that produced them. That feedback loop is the actual long-term return of The AI Operating System™.

Case Study: Structured Governance Success

A mid-sized manufacturing company — call it Meridian Manufacturing — approached AI adoption differently from its competitors. Rather than letting departments adopt platforms independently, leadership stood up a centralized evaluation process before any new AI tool could enter operational use. The goal was not to slow innovation. The goal was to make sure adoption aligned to measurable business priorities and survived contact with the operating environment.

Every proposed system was evaluated against four criteria: defined operational purpose, measurable business outcome, data governance exposure, and workflow integration impact. The company kept a centralized inventory, assigned named ownership to every platform, and ran a 45-minute quarterly review on cost, usage, performance, and business impact.

In the first quarter, the framework produced a visible cost: Meridian adopted AI roughly 20% more slowly than competitors who were buying tools on enthusiasm. By month nine, that picture had reversed. Meridian had eliminated three redundant subscriptions, killed an underperforming workflow tool before its renewal, and doubled investment in a single platform that the performance data showed was producing measurable results across three departments. Competitors operating without governance were carrying, on average, twice the AI subscription cost and an inventory that had grown faster than their visibility.

By month eighteen, Meridian's leadership could describe the AI environment in a sentence: every active tool, every cost line, every business outcome it supported, every renewal coming up in the next 90 days, every system carrying elevated risk. When the company won a regulated-industry client that quarter, the governance documentation was part of the procurement conversation — and the client said as much in the closing call.

The pattern this case represents is not unusual. The companies that build the operating discipline early do not slow down. They compound. Speed in AI adoption is not the same as advantage in AI adoption. Disciplined adoption is.

Note: Meridian Manufacturing is a composite example reflecting typical patterns observed across multiple client engagements. The specific details, 20% slower initial adoption, three retired subscriptions, 2× cost gap by month nine, represent realistic first-year outcomes when the framework is run consistently.

Your Complete Action Plan — Every Step, In Order, Starting Now

The implementation sequence is already defined. Each phase builds on the one before it; skipping ahead creates gaps that become operational problems later. The full implementation runs four to six weeks of focused effort, integrated into the normal business schedule. No technical team. No outside consultants. No capital investment. Operational discipline, recurring oversight, and leadership commitment.

Phase 1 — Establish Visibility (Week 1)

Build the centralized AI Tool Inventory. Every AI-enabled platform, embedded feature, automation, browser extension, and employee-adopted system in one document.

Reconcile against the last six months of credit card statements, bank records, and subscription expenses. Add anything not already captured.

Run the three discovery questions in a team conversation within the first five business days. Document everything. Do not react. The gap between leadership's awareness and what employees disclose is the first measure of shadow AI inside the business.

Phase 2 — Financial & Performance Control (Weeks 2–3)

Complete the full AI Business Enablement Audit™ across all five dimensions. Produce the four core artifacts: inventory, cost-and-performance baseline, risk map, governance gap list.

Categorize every tool by business function and dependency tier. Flag redundancy. Calculate true AI spend (subscription + variable + integration + labor). That number becomes the operational baseline.

Within 30 days of the audit, execute the first round of cost decisions: cancel idle systems, consolidate redundancy, establish the AI spending ceiling.

Run the AI Performance Scorecard™ for every active tool. Calculate ROI on the highest-cost systems first. Establish benchmarks and review triggers.

Phase 3 — Governance & Risk Controls (Weeks 3–4)

Run the ten-question risk assessment for every active tool. Assign Low / Medium / High ratings. High-risk systems get documented mitigation plans with named owners and deadlines.

Tier-1 dependency systems get contingency planning: alternative vendor, transition timeline, operational impact, accountability owner.

Draft the three core governance documents: AI Usage Policy, Tool Approval Process, Data Access Protocol. Plain language. Two pages each, maximum.

Run the thirty-minute governance introduction meeting. Send the one-paragraph written summary within 24 hours. Add governance acknowledgment to onboarding.

Phase 4 — Alignment, Integration, Decision Discipline (Weeks 4–5)

Build the AI-to-Outcome Alignment Map™. Every active tool. Five columns. Three classifications (Aligned / Partial / Unaligned).

Address every Unaligned system within thirty days — define a real objective and put the system on a structured review, reassign it to a function where alignment can be established, or removes it.

Map the three to five workflows that matter most. Run the AI Integration Checklist™ for every tool-workflow combination. Have direct operational conversations with the employees whose work will change.

Finalize the AI Adoption Decision Framework™ as a one-page document. Retroactively run the framework against every active system. Build the Standing AI Adoption Policy™.

Phase 5 — Activate the Operating System (Weeks 5–6)

Schedule the monthly review as a recurring commitment. Same day each month. Twenty minutes. Calendar invite links to inventory, baseline, and dashboard.

Schedule the quarterly governance review. Same week each quarter. Forty-five minutes. Calendar invite links to Scorecard, Alignment Map, policies, risk assessments.

Schedule the annual review. Several hours. Aligned to annual strategic planning. Even months out — scheduling it now is what keeps it from being deferred.

Assign secondary inventory ownership. Distribute operational maintenance away from executive leadership only.

Develop the external governance statement. Three points. Plain language. Add to onboarding, proposals, service agreements where appropriate.

Add a standing AI governance update to recurring leadership meetings. Even a one-minute confirmation reinforces that AI is now a managed function.

The Advantage Comes from Running It

You now have a complete operating system for controlling AI, reducing risk, measuring performance, and producing measurable business value. Most companies operating today do not. Most companies operating a year from now still will not.

The framework is built. The work that remains is not.

Twelve months from now, the business will either be the first version of the two scenarios that opened this chapter, or it will be the second. The framework is the same in both cases. The companies will be the same size. The technology will be the same. The difference is whether the operating rhythm was run.

The AI Operating System™ was designed to produce exactly that discipline. Not a one-time cleanup. Not a temporary initiative. A permanent management capability, visibility, accountability, consistency, strategic control, those scales as AI continues expanding across the business and across the market.

The system is built.

The advantage comes from running it.

Begin.

Appendix

Appendix: Audit Templates and Worksheets

The seven worksheets that follow convert the frameworks introduced across Chapters 4 through 12 into practical, fillable forms. Each one is designed for repeated use. Most leadership teams will run the first iteration of these worksheets during the initial 90-day audit described in Chapter 3, then re-run them on the cadence established by the AI Operating Calendar™ in Chapter 12.

The five per-tool worksheets (Templates 1 through 4 and Template 6) are structured as one tool per page. Photocopy each form as many times as needed and complete one per AI tool in active use. The two checklist worksheets (Templates 5 and 7) consolidate fixed governance and review rhythms onto a single working page.

The worksheets are sequenced in the order a leadership team would typically work through them: inventory first, then cost, then performance, then risk, then governance, then alignment, then the recurring rhythm that holds the system together.

Download editable spreadsheet versions of all seven templates, plus a free 90-day audit guide, at SRJConsultingServices.com/books.

TEMPLATE 1

AI Tool Inventory Worksheet™

Use this worksheet to build a complete inventory of every AI tool, platform, browser extension, and embedded AI feature operating across your business. Complete one form per tool. Most leadership teams discover two to four times more tools than they expected. That discovery is the point. Run this worksheet first, before any other.

Photocopy this page as many times as needed, one form per AI tool.

Tool Name	
Department / Owner	
Function / Purpose	
Subscription Type	☐ *Individual* ☐ *Team* ☐ *Enterprise* ☐ *Free*
Monthly Cost	*$*
Data Sensitivity	☐ *Public* ☐ *Internal* ☐ *Confidential* ☐ *Regulated*
Approval Status	☐ *Approved* ☐ *Provisional* ☐ *Shadow*
Date Discovered	
Notes	

TEMPLATE 2

AI Cost Map Worksheet

For each tool, calculate the true total cost of ownership. The subscription cost is rarely the largest line. Indirect labor, integration cost, and variable usage charges typically add thirty to seventy percent to the subscription figure. Complete all cost lines before calculating the monthly total.

Photocopy this page as many times as needed, one form per AI tool.

Tool Name	
Direct Subscription	$ *per month*
Per-Seat Licenses	*seats* × $ = $
Variable Usage	$ *per month (average)*
Integration & Setup	$ *amortized monthly*
Indirect Labor	*hours* × $ = $
Other Costs	$
Total Monthly Cost	$
Annual Total	$
Notes	

TEMPLATE 3

AI Performance Scorecard™

Score each tool across the four performance dimensions, zero to twenty-five points per dimension, for a one hundred point total. Scores below sixty indicate a tool that is not earning its place. Scores between sixty and eighty indicate a tool worth keeping but worth examining. Scores above eighty indicate a tool producing measurable value. Re-score quarterly.

Photocopy this page as many times as needed, one form per AI tool.

Tool Name	
Time Savings (0–25)	*Score: Justification:*
Cost Impact (0–25)	*Score: Justification:*
Output Quality (0–25)	*Score: Justification:*
Strategic Contribution (0–25)	*Score: Justification:*
Total Score (0–100)	
Interpretation	*☐ Below 60 ☐ 60–80 ☐ Above 80*
Recommended Action	*☐ Retire ☐ Examine ☐ Expand*
Notes	

TEMPLATE 4

AI Operational Risk Assessment™

Classify each tool across the four operational risk categories. Mark each as Low, Medium, or High. Tools carrying two or more High classifications require immediate governance attention. Tools carrying any High classification require documented mitigation. Re-assess at every quarterly governance review.

Photocopy this page as many times as needed, one form per AI tool.

Tool Name	
Data Risk	☐ *Low* ☐ *Medium* ☐ *High* *Notes:*
Decision Risk	☐ *Low* ☐ *Medium* ☐ *High* *Notes:*
Vendor Dependency Risk	☐ *Low* ☐ *Medium* ☐ *High* *Notes:*
Compliance Risk	☐ *Low* ☐ *Medium* ☐ *High* *Notes:*
Overall Classification	☐ *Low* ☐ *Medium* ☐ *High*
Action Owner	
Target Completion	
Mitigation Required	

TEMPLATE 5

AI Governance Gap Analysis

Walk through each governance control and mark the current state. Most organizations in the first audit cycle will mark five to seven of the categories as None or Partial. Document the gap, assign an owner, and set a target close date. Re-run annually as a complete governance health check.

Photocopy this page as many times as needed, one form per AI tool.

Governance Control	State	Owner	Target
Written AI Policy	□N □P □C		
Approval Process for New Tools	□N □P □C		
Data Handling Standards	□N □P □C		
Accountability Assignment	□N □P □C		
Recurring Review Cadence	□N □P □C		
Vendor Management Standards	□N □P □C		
Incident Response Protocol	□N □P □C		
Employee Training	□N □P □C		
Shadow AI Detection	□N □P □C		
Output Review Procedures	□N □P □C		

Cost Approval Thresholds	☐N ☐P ☐C		
Annual Governance Review	☐N ☐P ☐C		

State key: N = None P = Partial C = Complete

TEMPLATE 6

Outcome Alignment Map™

For each tool in the inventory, document the specific business priority it serves, the measurable outcome that justifies its continued use, and the strategic tier it occupies. Tools in the Critical tier must be re-evaluated quarterly. Tools in the Operational tier semi-annually. Tools in the Supplemental tier annually or when costs change.

Photocopy this page as many times as needed, one form per AI tool.

Tool Name	
Business Priority Served	
Measurable Outcome	
Strategic Tier	☐ *Critical* ☐ *Operational* ☐ *Supplemental*
Next Re-evaluation	
Reviewed By	
Notes	

TEMPLATE 7

AI Operating Calendar™

Establish the recurring governance rhythm that converts the audit from a one-time exercise into a permanent management discipline. Schedule each review at a fixed date, assign an accountable owner, and document the expected output. The Calendar is the single most important worksheet in the Appendix. Without it, the framework collapses back into ad-hoc activity.

Photocopy this page as many times as needed, one form per AI tool.

Review Type	Cadence	Next Date	Owner
Monthly Inventory Review	*Monthly*		
Monthly Cost Review	*Monthly*		
Quarterly Performance Review	*Quarterly*		
Quarterly Risk Re-Assessment	*Quarterly*		
Quarterly Alignment Review	*Quarterly*		
Semi-Annual Vendor Review	*Semi-Annual*		
Annual Governance Policy Review	*Annual*		
Annual Full Audit Re-Run	*Annual*		
Triggered Incident Review	*As Needed*		

Using the Worksheets

The seven worksheets are designed to work as a sequenced system, not as independent tools. Template 1 (Inventory) feeds Templates 2 through 6. Template 7 (Operating Calendar) holds the rhythm that triggers all the others.

Most leadership teams complete the first iteration across two weeks of focused work, then settle into the recurring rhythm captured in the Calendar. The cumulative time investment after the first cycle is approximately four to six hours of leadership time per quarter, less than the time most companies already spend on AI-related decisions made without a framework.

Updated spreadsheet versions of all seven worksheets, plus a free 90-day audit guide, are available at SRJConsultingServices.com/books.

References

Abonamah, A. A., & Abdelhamid, N. (2024). Managerial insights for AI/ML implementation: a playbook for successful organizational integration. *Discover Artificial Intelligence, 4.*

Agrawal, K. (2023). Towards Adoption of Generative AI in Organizational Settings. *Journal of Computer Information Systems, 64*(5), 636-651.

Ahmed, Q. U. A., Ahmed, A., & Sandhu, K. Y. (2025). Artificial Intelligence to Business Performance: A Mediation Model of Technology Adoption Readiness and Corporate Governance. *Journal of Asian Development Studies.*

Al-Khatib, A. W. (2023). Drivers of generative artificial intelligence to fostering exploitative and exploratory innovation: A TOE framework. *Technology in Society.*

Alzahrani, S. (2025). Assessing artificial intelligence and advanced analytics adoption: A technological, organizational, and environmental perspective. *Edelweiss Applied Science and Technology, 9*(7), 312-325.

Baabdullah, A. M. (2024). The precursors of AI adoption in business: Towards efficient decision-making and functional performance. *International Journal of Information Management, 75*, 102745.

Badghish, S., & Soomro, Y. A. (2024). Artificial Intelligence Adoption by SMEs to Achieve Sustainable Business Performance: Application of Technology–Organization–Environment Framework. *Sustainability, 16*(5), 1864.

Chandrakanth, L., & Engineer, K. S. (2025). Overcoming Adoption Barriers: Strategies for Scalable AI Transformation in Enterprises. *Journal of Informatics Education and Research, 5*(2).

Chatterjee, S., Rana, N. P., Dwivedi, Y. K., & Baabdullah, A. (2021). Understanding AI adoption in manufacturing and production firms using an integrated TAM-TOE model. *Technological Forecasting and Social Change, 170*, 120880.

Chen, J., & Tajdini, S. (2024). A moderated model of artificial intelligence adoption in firms and its effects on their performance. *Information Technology and Management, 26*, 407-419.

Dey, D., & Ghose, D. (2025). Integrating AI Adoption Frameworks with Digital Maturity Models: Strategic Pathways in a Rapidly Evolving Technological Landscape. *Journal of Contemporary Business Research, 1*, 156-170.

Dey, P., Chowdhury, S., Abadie, A., Yaroson, E., & Sarkar, S. (2023). Artificial intelligence-driven supply chain resilience in Vietnamese manufacturing small- and medium-sized enterprises. *International Journal of Production Research, 62*(15), 5417-5456.

Dora, M., Kumar, A., Mangla, S., Pant, A., & Kamal, M. (2021). Critical success factors influencing artificial intelligence adoption in food supply chains. *International Journal of Production Research, 60*(14), 4621-4640.

Dreyling, R., Lemmik, J., Tammet, T., & Pappel, I. (2024). An Artificial Intelligence Maturity Model for the Public Sector: A Design Science Approach. *TalTech Journal of European Studies, 14*(2), 217-239.

Felemban, H., Sohail, M., & Ruikar, K. (2024). Exploring the Readiness of Organisations to Adopt Artificial Intelligence. *Buildings, 14*(8), 2460.

Gottumukkala, S. (2025). Decoding the Organisational AI Adoption: What Do Theories and Frameworks Reveal? *Journal of International Commercial Law and Technology.*

Hansen, H., Lillesund, E., Mikalef, P., & Altwaijry, N. (2024). Understanding Artificial Intelligence Diffusion through an AI Capability Maturity Model. *Information Systems Frontiers, 26*, 2147–2163.

Hao, X., Demir, E., & Eyers, D. (2025). Critical success and failure factors in the AI lifecycle: a knowledge graph-based ontological study. *Journal of Modelling in Management.*

Hassan, M., Kushniruk, A., & Borycki, E. (2023). Barriers to and Facilitators of Artificial Intelligence Adoption in Health Care: Scoping Review. *JMIR Human Factors, 11*, e48633.

Heger, A. K., Passi, S., Dhanorkar, S., Kahn, Z., Wang, R., & Vorvoreanu, M. (2025). Towards a Responsible AI Organizational Maturity Model. *Proceedings of the ACM on Human-Computer Interaction, 9*(CSCW1), 1-33.

Hržica, R., Debelak, K., & Pevcin, P. (2025). A Dual-Level Model of AI Readiness in the Public Sector: Merging Organizational and Individual Factors Using TOE and UTAUT. *Systems, 13*, 705.

Jöhnk, J., Weißert, M., & Wyrtki, K. (2020). Ready or Not, AI Comes—An Interview Study of Organizational AI Readiness Factors. *Business & Information Systems Engineering, 63*(1), 5-20.

Kalleparambil, S. A., & Akoum, M. (2025). AI Organisational Readiness for SMEs: A Tailored Model for AI Adoption Success. *Journal of Information & Knowledge Management, 24*.

Kar, A. K., & Kushwaha, A. (2021). Facilitators and Barriers of Artificial Intelligence Adoption in Business – Insights from Opinions Using Big Data Analytics. *Information Systems Frontiers, 25*(3), 1351-1374.

Kucevic, E., Grünewald, F., & Schanz, N. (2024). Towards a Simplified AI Adoption Framework: Success Factors for the Implementation of Artificial Intelligence Information Systems. *Springer Nature*, 88-106.

Kumar, A., Shankar, A., Hollebeek, L., Behl, A., & Lim, W. M. (2025). Generative artificial intelligence (GenAI) revolution: A deep dive into GenAI adoption. *Journal of Business Research*.

Kurup, S., & Gupta, V. (2022). Factors Influencing the AI Adoption in Organizations. *Metamorphosis: A Journal of Management Research, 21*(2), 129-139.

Lada, S., et al. (2023). Determining Factors Related to Artificial Intelligence (AI) Adoption Among Malaysia's Small and Medium-Sized Businesses. *Journal of Open Innovation: Technology, Market, and Complexity*.

Lutfiani, N., Sembiring, I., Setyawan, I., Setiawan, A., Rahardja, U., & Sulistio, S. (2025). Exploring the Relationship between Artificial Intelligence and Business Performance. *IJCCS (Indonesian Journal of Computing and Cybernetics Systems).*

Madanchian, M., & Taherdoost, H. (2025). Ethical theories, governance models, and strategic frameworks for responsible AI adoption and organizational success. *Frontiers in Artificial Intelligence, 8.*

Neumann, O., Guirguis, K., & Steiner, R. (2022). Exploring artificial intelligence adoption in public organizations: a comparative case study. *Public Management Review, 26*(1), 114-141.

Oyekunle, D., & Boohene, D. (2024). DIGITAL TRANSFORMATION POTENTIAL: THE ROLE OF ARTIFICIAL INTELLIGENCE IN BUSINESS. *International Journal of Professional Business Review, 9*(3).

Papagiannidis, E., et al. (2022). Toward AI Governance: Identifying Best Practices and Potential Barriers and Outcomes. *Information Systems Frontiers, 25*(1), 123-141.

Patnaik, P., & Bakkar, M. (2024). Exploring Determinants Influencing Artificial Intelligence Adoption, Reference to Diffusion of Innovation Theory. *Technology in Society.*

Phuoc, N. V. (2022). The Critical Factors Impacting Artificial Intelligence Applications Adoption in Vietnam: A Structural Equation Modeling Analysis. *Economies, 10*(6).

Polisetty, A., et al. (2023). What Determines AI Adoption in Companies? Mixed-Method Evidence. *Journal of Computer Information Systems, 64*(3), 370-387.

Poon, E. G., et al. (2025). Adoption of artificial intelligence in healthcare: survey of health system priorities, successes, and challenges. *Journal of the American Medical Informatics Association (JAMIA), 32*, 1093–1100.

Priya, S. S., et al. (2022). Modelling the factors in the adoption of artificial intelligence in Indian management institutes. *foresight.*

Pumplun, L., Tauchert, C., & Heidt, M. (2019). A New Organizational Chassis for Artificial Intelligence - Exploring Organizational Readiness Factors. *ECIS 2019 Proceedings*.

Sadiq, R. B., et al. (2021). Artificial intelligence maturity model: a systematic literature review. *PeerJ Computer Science, 7*, e661.

Sánchez, E., Calderón, R., & Herrera, F. (2025). Artificial Intelligence Adoption in SMEs: Survey Based on TOE–DOI Framework, Primary Methodology and Challenges. *Applied Sciences, 15*(12), 6465.

Song, Y., Qiu, X., & Liu, J. (2025). The Impact of Artificial Intelligence Adoption on Organizational Decision-Making: An Empirical Study Based on the Technology Acceptance Model in Business Management. *Systems, 13*(8), 683.

Soomro, R., et al. (2025). A SEM–ANN analysis to examine impact of artificial intelligence technologies on sustainable performance of SMEs. *Scientific Reports, 15*, 3568.

Tursunbayeva, A., & Gal, H. C. B. (2024). Adoption of artificial intelligence: A TOP framework-based checklist for digital leaders. *Business Horizons*.

Uren, V., & Edwards, J. (2023). Technology readiness and the organizational journey towards AI adoption: An empirical study. *International Journal of Information Management, 68*, 102588.

Westover, J. H. (2025). Sustainable AI Transformation: A Critical Framework for Organizational Resilience and Long-Term Viability. *Sustainability, 17*(21), 9822.

Yablonsky, S. (2021). AI-driven platform enterprise maturity: from human led to machine governed. *Kybernetes, 50*(9), 2753-2789.

Companion Materials

Every framework, diagram, and worksheet in this book is available online for your use, free, at https://srjconsultingservices.com/books/ai-business-services/the-ai-business-enablement-audit/

The companion library includes:

The seven audit worksheets as editable spreadsheets, ready to populate during your audit. Compatible with Excel, Google Sheets, and any standard spreadsheet application.

The complete chapter graphics library, organized by chapter from Introduction through Conclusion. Every diagram, framework, and chart from this book is available as an individual file you can preview and download, ready to drop into your slide decks, board presentations, internal memos, and team training materials.

The standalone Appendix Introduction and closing guidance as Word documents, for organizations that want to brief their teams or distribute the methodology internally.

All companion materials are made available without restriction for legitimate business use within the organization that purchased this book. If you are running this audit at your company, share the templates with your team. If you are presenting the frameworks to your board, use the graphics. The materials exist to make the work easier.

For additional resources including AI governance frameworks, executive workshops, and advisory engagements, visit SRJConsultingServices.com.

Continuing the Work

The **AI Business Enablement Audit**™ is the first volume in *The Operating Discipline for AI Library*™ , a nine-volume canon on running AI as a permanent business function. Each volume addresses one of the disciplines a leadership team has to install, in roughly the order a serious organization needs them. The canon is organized into two pillars. The first, AI Business Services, takes a leadership team from its first audit through full operating maturity. The second, AI Risk Governance & Security, covers the protection and exposure work, including the three security disciplines that AI has structurally changed.

The full canon is below. Each title is also a service line at SRJ Consulting & Services, paired with the working templates and frameworks that move the discipline from a printed page into an operating rhythm.

Pillar I — AI Business Services

https://srjconsultingservices.com/books/ai-business-services/

Volume **I. The AI Business Enablement Audit**™**.** The diagnostic foundation of the canon. A structured, plain-English evaluation of how AI is operating across a business, what it is costing fully loaded, and whether it is producing measurable outcomes. https://srjconsultingservices.com/books/ai-business-services/the-ai-business-enablement-audit/

Volume **II. The AI Readiness & Performance Assessment**™**.** A forward-looking evaluation of whether the organization is prepared to scale AI responsibly, covering workflow maturity, data quality, internal controls, and the measurement infrastructure AI depends on. https://srjconsultingservices.com/books/ai-business-services/the-ai-readiness-performance-assessment/

Volume **III. The AI Risk & Governance Review™.** AI introduces risk at the data, decision, and vendor layers. This book establishes governance structures proportionate to the organization's size and risk profile, without slowing the operations that depend on AI. https://srjconsultingservices.com/books/ai-business-services/the-ai-risk-governance-review/

Volume **IV. The AI Efficiency & Process Optimization™.** Once AI is understood and governed, this book turns to operational effectiveness. Repeatable processes, reduced manual effort, and labor savings that are genuinely captured. The closing book of Pillar I. https://srjconsultingservices.com/books/ai-business-services/the-ai-efficiency-process-optimization/

Pillar II — AI Risk Governance & Security

https://srjconsultingservices.com/books/ai-risk-governance-security/

Volume V. The AI IT Security Audit™. A CISO-grade audit framework for proving AI exposure is known, controlled, and governed. An exposure map, a remediation roadmap, a regulatory crosswalk, and a board briefing across the six security domains. https://srjconsultingservices.com/books/ai-risk-governance-security/the-ai-it-security-audit/

Volume VI. The AI IT Security Implementation & Strategy™. The operating manual for proving AI risk is governed. Ratified policies, an integrated risk register, a regulatory crosswalk, and board reporting that survives the question. A discipline to operate, not a project to complete. https://srjconsultingservices.com/books/ai-risk-governance-security/the-ai-it-security-implementation-strategy/

Volume VII. Secure by Design in the Age of AI™. Engineering velocity is up an order of magnitude. Security review capacity is not. This book defines the Dual-Impedance Problem and the five-framework operating model that closes it for organizations shipping AI-enabled products. https://srjconsultingservices.com/books/ai-risk-governance-security/the-secure-by-design/

Volume VIII. Application Security in the Age of AI™. Every application security tool ever built was built on the premise that an application produces the same output for the same input. AI invalidated that. This book defines the Runtime Determinism Gap and the program model for application security in a world where applications no longer behave deterministically. https://srjconsultingservices.com/books/ai-risk-governance-security/the-application-security/

Volume IX. Cloud and Infrastructure Security in the Age of AI™. Cloud security was built on the premise that every meaningful action could be traced to an accountable human. AI broke that. This book defines the Sovereignty Problem and the cloud security operating model for an era where most actors inside the infrastructure are not human. https://srjconsultingservices.com/books/ai-risk-governance-security/the-cloud-infrastructure-security/

Together, these nine volumes form a complete operating discipline. They are designed to be read in order by a leadership team that is serious about installing AI as a managed function inside the business, and to be referenced by name as the work moves from audit to assessment to governance to optimization to security. Each volume stands on its own. Read together, they form the canon.

More information can be found at https://srjconsultingservices.com/books/.

About the Author

Stephen R. Jordan is the founder of SRJ Consulting & Services LLC an operator-led AI advisory practice based in Frisco, Texas. His work helps executives establish governance, oversight, and operational discipline around artificial intelligence as a managed business function, not an experimental tool.

Jordan's professional background spans accounting, enterprise technology, cybersecurity, operational systems management, and risk governance. Over the course of a career that includes leadership, consulting, and advisory roles across multiple industries, he has worked extensively in operational oversight, business systems management, enterprise security, incident response, governance frameworks, and technology implementation. His experience includes work involving operational risk management, infrastructure security, compliance oversight, and business process improvement inside complex enterprise environments.

Prior to founding SRJ Consulting & Services LLC in 2023, Jordan held senior consulting, operational, and security roles at organizations including Citi, Optiv, Intel, and McAfee. His engagements spanned enterprise technology, cybersecurity operations, governance processes, and systems management, with recurring focus on operational risk, infrastructure security, compliance oversight, and the management infrastructure required to keep complex enterprise environments running as designed.

Jordan earned a Bachelor of Business Administration in Accounting from West Texas A&M University and later completed graduate studies involving political science, commerce, computer science, and educational media and technology. His multidisciplinary background contributed to the operational and governance-focused perspective reflected throughout The AI Operating System™ framework.

Through his work with business owners and organizational leadership teams, Jordan recognized that many companies were adopting artificial intelligence faster than they were developing the operational systems required to govern it effectively. That observation ultimately became the foundation for The AI Operating System™, the AI Business Enablement Audit™, and the broader governance and operational frameworks introduced throughout this book.

Today, Jordan works with organizations seeking to improve visibility, governance, operational discipline, cost control, and measurable performance across artificial intelligence initiatives and business technology environments. His work focuses on helping businesses manage AI intentionally through structured operational systems rather than fragmented adoption and uncontrolled experimentation.

For additional resources, AI governance frameworks, executive workshops, and advisory engagements, visit SRJConsultingServices.com.